Apache Jakarta Tomcat

JAMES GOODWILL

Apress™

Apache Jakarta Tomcat

ISBN (pbk): 1-893115-36-4

Printed and bound in the United States of America 2345678910

Editorial Directors: Dan Appleman, Gary Cornell, Jason Gilmore, Karen Watterson
Technical Reviewer: Aaron Bandell
Project Managers: Alexa Stuart, Erin Mulligan
Developmental and Copy Editor: Tom Gillen, Gillen Editorial, Inc.
Production Editor: Sofia Marchant
Compositor: Impressions Book and Journal Services, Inc.
Indexer: Ron Strauss
Cover Designer: Tom Debolski
Managing Editor: Grace Wong
Marketing Manager: Stephanie Rodriguez

Distributed to the book trade in the United States by Springer-Verlag New York, Inc.,175 Fifth Avenue, New York, NY, 10010
and outside the United States by Springer-Verlag GmbH & Co. KG, Tiergartenstr. 17, 69112 Heidelberg, Germany

In the United States, phone 1-800-SPRINGER, email orders@springer-ny.com, or visit http://www.springer-ny.com.
Outside the United States, fax +49 6221 345229, email orders@springer.de, or visit http://www.springer.de.

For information on translations, please contact Apress directly at 901 Grayson Street, Suite 204, Berkeley, CA 94710.
Phone 510-549-5930, fax: 510-549-5939, email info@apress.com, or visit http://www.apress.com.

The source code for this book is available to readers at http://www.apress.com in the Downloads section. You will need to answer questions pertaining to this book to successfully download the code.

Dedication

To my girls Christy, Abby, and Emma.

Contents at a Glance

Contents

Acknowledgments

I would like to begin this text by thanking the people who made this book what it is today. They are the people who took my words and shaped them into something that I hope will help you use the Tomcat container to its fullest. Of these people, I would like to explicitly thank Jason Gilmore, Alexa Stuart, Erin Mulligan, Aaron Bandell, Tom Gillen, Sofia Marchant, Ron Strauss, and Grace Wong. Each and every person made this book what it is today.

On a closer note, I would like to thank everyone at my company, Virtuas Solutions, LLC, for their support while I was completing this text. The entire, "UNREAL", staff contributed by picking up my assignments when my plate was too full.

Finally, the most important contributors to this book are my wife Christy, and our daughters Abby and Emma. They are the ones who really sacrificed during the development of this text, especially when I walked in the room discussing another Tomcat beta release. They are the ones who deserve the credit for this book. With their support, I can do anything.

Introduction

WHEN I BEGAN THIS text, Tomcat was at version 4.0 beta 1. It has come a long way between beta 1 and the final release, and each release included additional functionality and improved performance. The Tomcat team has really done a great job. They have successfully created a product that is on par with, or above, all other Java Web application containers on the market, whether commercial or open source.

As with any open source project, new changes were being added all of the time. In this text, I have tried to cover the components of the Tomcat container that I thought would be most relevant, but, as I mentioned earlier, new releases will have additional functionality. As you progress through this text, feel free to send comments about areas that you would like to see in future releases. My goal is to make this text the only Tomcat reference you need in your library. That is enough from me. I hope you enjoy this book.

About the Author

James Goodwill is the co-founder and Chief Technology Officer at Virtuas Solutions, L.L.C., located in Denver, Colorado. He has extensive experience in designing and architecting e-business applications. James authored the best-selling Java titles *Developing Java Servlets* and *Pure JavaServer Pages* and is also a regular columnist on the Java community Web site, OnJava.com.

About the Technical Reviewer

TECHNICAL WRITER Aaron Bandell has been a professional in the software industry for six years. Most recently, Aaron has spent his time architecting J2EE applications. He aspires to one day develop a process that will allow him to work while on the ski slopes.

CHAPTER 1

Jakarta Tomcat

In this chapter, we

- Introduce the Jakarta Tomcat server
- Describe the Jakarta Tomcat architecture
- Define Java Web applications
- Discuss the requirements for installing and configuring Tomcat
- Describe the steps of installing and configuring Tomcat
- Test your Tomcat installation

The Jakarta Tomcat Server

The Jakarta Tomcat server is an open source, Java-based Web application container that was created to run servlet and JavaServer Page Web applications. It exists under the Apache-Jakarta subproject, where it is supported and enhanced by a group of volunteers from the open source Java community.

The Tomcat server has become the reference implementation for both the servlet and JSP specifications. It is very stable and has all of the features of a commercial Web application container. Tomcat also provides additional functionality that makes it a great choice for developing a complete Web application solution. Some of the additional features provided by Tomcat—other than being open source and free—include the Tomcat Manager application, specialized realm implementations, and Tomcat valves.

The Tomcat Manager Web Application

The Tomcat Manager Web application is packaged with the Tomcat server. It is installed in the context path of `/manager` and provides the basic functionality to manage Web applications running in the Tomcat server. Some of the provided functionality includes the ability to install, start, stop, remove, and report on Web applications.

Specialized Realm Implementations

Tomcat provides two methods for protecting resources. The first `authentication` implementation provided with Tomcat is a memory realm. The class that implements the memory realm is `org.apache.catalina.realm.MemoryRealm`. The `MemoryRealm` class uses a simple XML file as a container of users.

The second authentication implementation included with Tomcat is a JDBC realm. A `JDBCRealm` class is much like the `MemoryRealm`, with the exception of where it stores its collection of users. A `JDBCRealm` stores all of its users in a user-defined, JDBC-compliant database.

Tomcat Valves

Tomcat valves are a new technology introduced with Tomcat 4. They allow you to associate an instance of a Java class with a particular Catalina container. Valves are proprietary to Tomcat and cannot, at this time, be used in a different servlet/JSP container.

Further Information

Throughout this text, we discuss all of these Tomcat-specific features and some other features that are common to all Web application containers. More information about Tomcat can be found on its homepage:

```
http://jakarta.apache.org/tomcat/index.html
```

Figure 1-1 shows the Tomcat homepage.

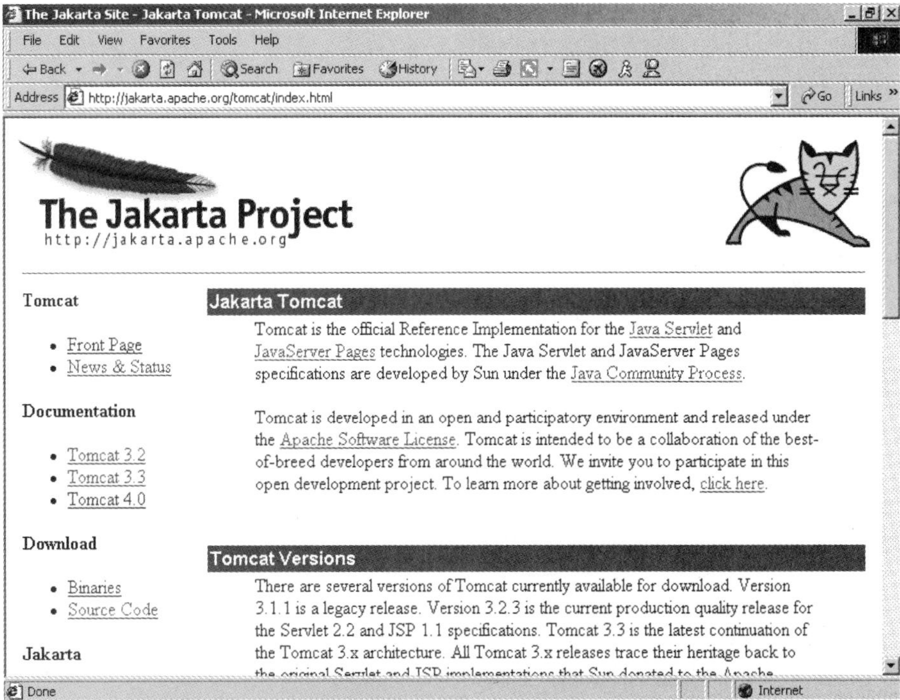

Figure 1-1. The Tomcat homepage

You can also subscribe to the Tomcat mailing lists, which can be found at the following URL:

```
http://jakarta.apache.org/site/mail2.html
```

This page contains all of the mailing lists controlled by the Apache Jakarta project. Once you are on the mailing lists page, scroll down until you find the Tomcat lists and select the list that you would like to subscribe to. Figure 1-2 shows the mailing list options for Tomcat.

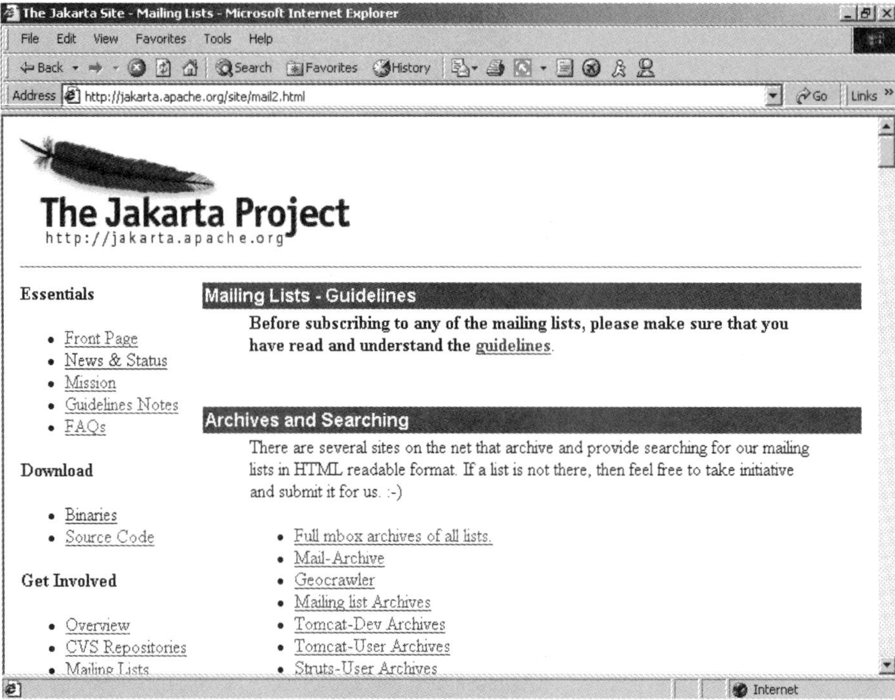

Figure 1-2. The Tomcat mailing lists

The Architecture of Tomcat

Tomcat 4 is a complete rewrite of its ancestors. At the core of this rewrite is the Catalina servlet engine, which acts as the top-level container for all Tomcat instances.

With this rewrite of Tomcat comes an entirely new architecture composed of a grouping of application containers, each with a specific role. The sum of all of these containers makes up an instance of a Catalina engine. The following code snippet provides an XML representation of the relationships between the different Tomcat containers:

```
<Server>

  <Service>

    <Connector />

    <Engine>
```

```
      <Host>

        <Context>
        </Context>

      </Host>

    </Engine>

  </Service>

</Server>
```

This instance can be broken down into a set of containers including a server, a service, a connector, an engine, a host, and a context. By default, each of these containers is configured using the `server.xml` file, which we describe later in more detail.

The Server

The first container element referenced in this snippet is the `<Server>` element. It represents the entire Catalina servlet engine and is used as a top-level element for a single Tomcat instance. The `<Server>` element may contain one or more `<Service>` containers.

The Service

The next container element is the `<Service>` element, which holds a collection of one or more `<Connector>` elements that share a single `<Engine>` element. *N*-number of `<Service>` elements may be nested inside a single `<Server>` element.

The Connector

The next type of element is the `<Connector>` element, which defines the class that does the actual handling requests and responses to and from a calling client application.

The Engine

The third container element is the `<Engine>` element. Each defined `<Service>` can have only one `<Engine>` element, and this single `<Engine>` component handles all requests received by all of the defined `<Connector>` components defined by a parent service.

The Host

The `<Host>` element defines the virtual hosts that are contained in each instance of a Catalina `<Engine>`. Each `<Host>` can be a parent to one or more Web applications, with each being represented by a `<Context>` component.

The Context

The `<Context>` element is the most commonly used container in a Tomcat instance. Each `<Context>` element represents an individual Web application that is running within a defined `<Host>`. There is no limit to the number of contexts that can be defined within a `<Host>`.

Java Web Applications

The main function of the Tomcat server is to act as a container for Java Web applications. Therefore, before we can begin our Tomcat-specific discussions, a brief introduction as to exactly what Web applications are is in order. The concept of a Web application was introduced with the release of the Java servlet specification 2.2. According to this specification, "a Web Application is a collection of servlets, html pages, classes, and other resources that can be bundled and run on multiple containers from multiple vendors." What this really means is that a Web application is a container that can hold any combination of the following list of objects:

- servlets
- JavaServer pages (JSPs)
- utility classes
- static documents including HTML, images, and so on

- client-side classes
- meta-information describing the Web application

One of the main characteristics of a Web application is its relationship to the ServletContext. Each Web application has one and only one ServletContext. This relationship is controlled by the servlet container and guarantees that no two Web applications will clash when accessing objects in the ServletContext. We discuss this relationship in much more detail in Chapter 3 ("Servlets, JSPs, and the ServletContext").

The Directory Structure

The container that holds the components of a Web application is the directory structure in which it exists. The first step in creating a Web application is creating this directory structure. Table 1-1 contains a sample Web application, named /apress, and a description of what each of its directories should contain. Each one of these directories should be created from the <SERVER_ROOT> of the Web application container. An example of a <SERVER_ROOT> using Tomcat would be /jakarta-tomcat/webapps.

Table 1-1. The Directories of a Web Application

DIRECTORY	DESCRIPTION
/apress	The root directory of the Web application. All JSP and HTML files should be stored here.
/apress/WEB-INF	Contains all resources related to the application that are not in the document root of the application. This is where your Web application deployment descriptor is located (defined in the next section). Note that the WEB-INF directory is not part of the public document. No files contained in this directory can be requested directly by a client.
/apress/WEB-INF/classes	Where servlet and utility classes are located
/apress/WEB-INF/lib	Contains Java Archive files that the Web application is dependent upon. For example, this is where you would place a JAR file that contained a JDBC driver or JSP tag library.

As you look over the contents of the Web application's directory structure, notice that Web applications allow for compiled objects to be stored in both the

/WEB-INF/classes and /WEB-INF/lib directories. Of these two, the class loader loads classes from the /classes directory first, followed by the JARs that are stored in the /lib directory. If duplicate objects in both the /classes and /lib directories exist, the objects in the /classes directory take precedence.

The Deployment Descriptor

At the heart of all Web applications is a deployment descriptor that is an XML file named web.xml. The deployment descriptor is located in the /<SERVER_ROOT>/applicationname/WEB-INF/ directory. It describes configuration information for the entire Web application. For our application, the web.xml file is in the /<SERVER_ROOT>/apress /WEB-INF/ directory. The information that is contained in the deployment descriptor includes the following elements:

- servlet definitions
- servlet initialization parameters
- session configuration parameters
- servlet/JSP Mappings
- MIME type mappings
- security configuration parameters
- a welcome file list
- a list of error pages
- resource and environment variable definitions

The following code snippet contains a limited example of a Web application deployment descriptor. As we move through this book, we will be looking at the web.xml file and its elements in much more detail.

```
<web-app>
  <display-name>The APress App</display-name>
  <session-timeout>30</session-timeout>
  <servlet>
    <servlet-name>TestServlet</servlet-name>
    <servlet-class>com.apress.TestServlet</servlet-class>
```

```
    <load-on-startup>1</load-on-startup>
    <init-param>
      <param-name>name</param-name>
      <param-value>value</param-value>
    </init-param>
  </servlet>
</web-app>
```

In this example, we are setting three application-level elements, the first of which is the `<display-name>`. This element simply describes the name of the Web application. It is functionally ineffective.

The second Web application-level element is the `<session-timeout>` element, which controls the lifetime of the application's `HttpSession` object. The `<session-timeout>` value that we have used above tells the JSP/servlet container that the `HttpSession` object will become invalid after 30 minutes of inactivity.

The last application-level element that we have defined is the `<servlet>` element, which defines a servlet and its properties. We will further define the `<servlet>` elements when we discuss deploying servlets and JSPs to Tomcat in Chapter 2 ("Deploying Web Applications to Tomcat").

Packaging

Now that you know what a Web application is, you need to package it for deployment. The standard method for packaging Web applications is to use a Web archive (WAR) file, which you can create by using Java's archiving tool jar. An example of this would be to change to the root directory of your Web application and type the following command:

```
jar cvf apress.war .
```

This command produces an archive file named `apress.war` that contains your entire Web application. Now you can deploy your Web application by simply distributing this file, which we will cover in Chapter 2.

Requirements for Installing and Configuring Tomcat

Before we get started performing the tasks outlined by this chapter, you need to download the items listed in Table 1-2.

Table 1-2. Tomcat Requirements

NAME	LOCATION
Tomcat 4	`http://jakarta.apache.org/site/binindex.html`
JDK 1.3 Standard Edition	`http://java.sun.com/j2se/1.3/`

Installing and Configuring Tomcat

In this section, we install Tomcat as a standalone server, which means that Tomcat will service all requests, including static content, JSPs, and servlets.

To install and configure Tomcat, first download the packages from the previously listed locations. You should choose the appropriate downloads based on your operating system. (We cover the steps involved in installing to both NT/2000 and Linux.)

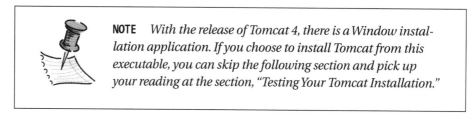

NOTE *With the release of Tomcat 4, there is a Window installation application. If you choose to install Tomcat from this executable, you can skip the following section and pick up your reading at the section, "Testing Your Tomcat Installation."*

Manually Installing to Windows NT/2000

The first installation we will be performing is for Windows NT/2000. The first thing you need to do is install the JDK. For this example, I am installing the JDK to drive `D:`, so therefore my `JAVA_HOME` directory is `D:\jdk1.3`.

NOTE *Make sure you follow the instructions included with your OS-appropriate JDK.*

Now you need to extract the Tomcat server to the directory where you want it to run. Again, I am installing to drive `D:`, which makes my `TOMCAT_HOME` directory `D:\jakarta-tomcat`.

NOTE *Tomcat does not come packaged with any install scripts. Therefore, extraction equals installation.*

After you have extracted Tomcat, you need to add two environment variables to the NT/2000 system: `JAVA_HOME`, which is the root directory of your JDK installation, and `TOMCAT_HOME`, which is the root directory of your Tomcat installation. To do this under NT/2000, perform the following steps:

1. Open the NT/2000 control panel. You should see an image similar to that shown in Figure 1-3.

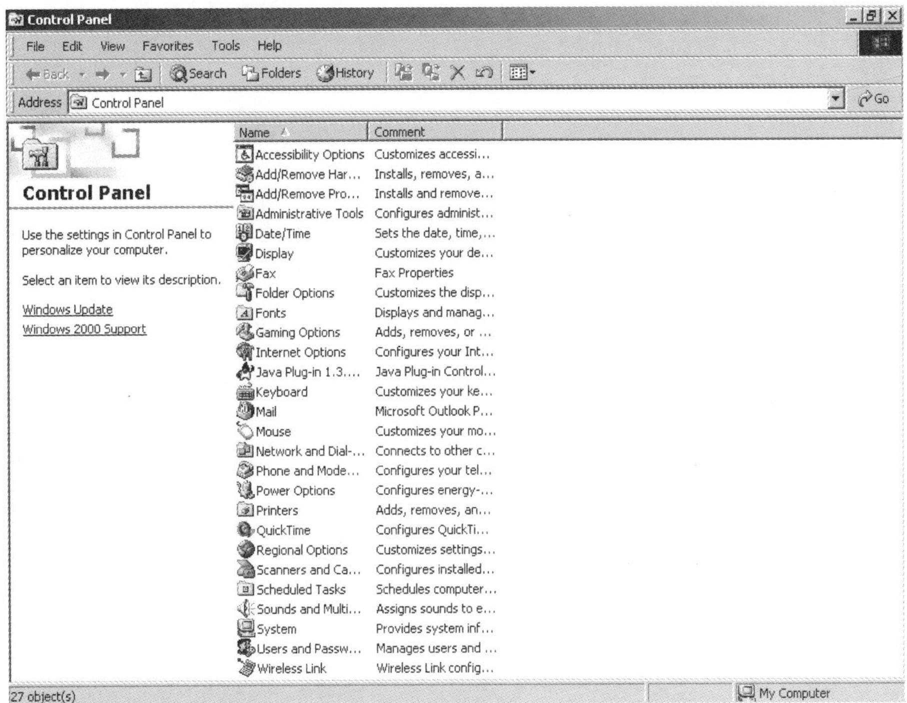

Figure 1-3. NT/2000 control panel

2. Now start the NT/2000 system application and click on the Advanced tab. You should see a screen similar to that shown in Figure 1-4.

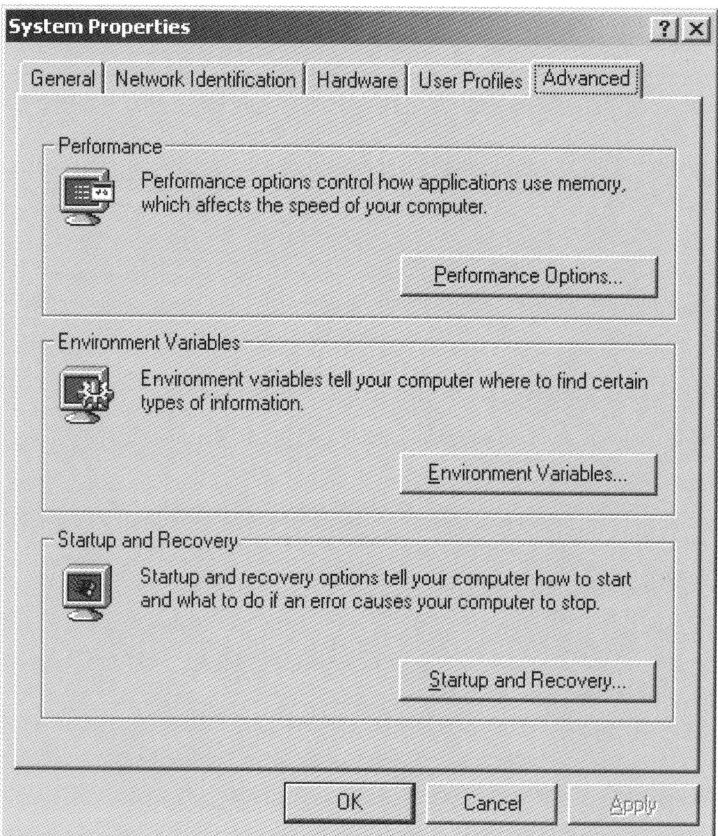

Figure 1-4. NT/2000 system application

3. Next, click on the Environment Variables button. You will see a screen similar to that shown in Figure 1-5.

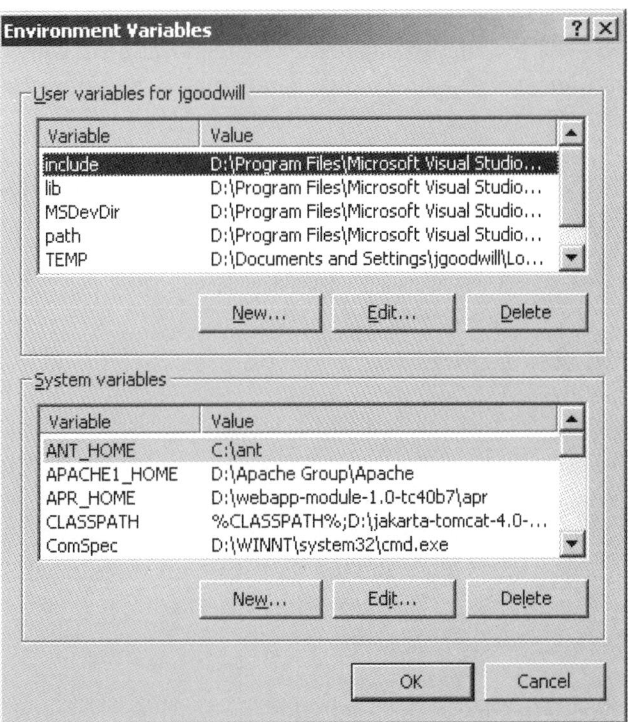

Figure 1-5. Environment variables dialog box

4. Now, click on the New button on the System Variables section of the Environment Variables dialog box. Add a variable named `JAVA_HOME` and set its value to the location of your JDK installation. Figure 1-6 shows the settings associated with my installation.

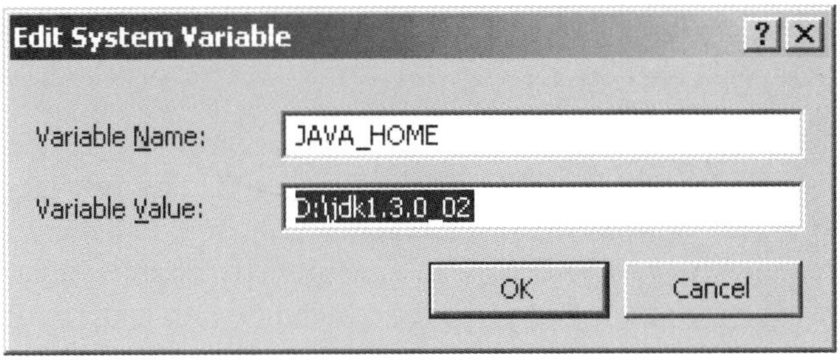

Figure 1-6. `JAVA_HOME` *environment settings*

5. Your final step should be to repeat Step 4, but this time using `TOMCAT_HOME` for the variable name and the location of your Tomcat installation as the value. For my installation, I am setting the value to `D:\jakarta-tomcat`.

That is all there is to it. If you are not going to perform a Linux installation, you should skip the following section "Installing to Linux" and move on to the section "Testing Your Tomcat Installation."

Installing to Linux

A Linux installation is a much simpler process compared to a Windows installation. The first thing you need to do is install the downloaded JDK. It is assumed that the JDK is installed to `/user/java/jdk1.3.0_02`.

After the JDK has been installed, you need to set the `JAVA_HOME` environment variable. To do this under Linux, find the shell that you are using in Table 1-3 and type the matching command. You need to replace `/user/java/jdk1.3.0_02` with the root location of your JDK installation.

Table 1-3. `JAVA_HOME` *Environment Commands*

SHELL	JAVA_HOME
bash	`JAVA_HOME=/user/java/jdk1.3.0_02;export JAVA_HOME`
tsh	`setenv JAVA_HOME /user/java/jdk1.3.0_02`

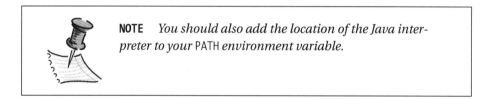

NOTE *You should also add the location of the Java interpreter to your* `PATH` *environment variable.*

You now need to extract the Tomcat server to a directory of your choosing. This directory will become the `TOMCAT_HOME` directory. For this installation, we assume that Tomcat is installed to `/var/tomcat`.

The last step is to set the `TOMCAT_HOME` environment variable. Find the shell that you are using in Table 1-4 and type the matching command. You need to replace `/var/tomcat` with the directory of your Tomcat installation.

Table 1-4. TOMCAT_HOME *Environment Commands*

SHELL	TOMCAT_HOME
bash	TOMCAT_HOME=/var/tomcat;export TOMCAT_HOME
tsh	setenv TOMCAT _HOME /var/tomcat

And that is all there is to the Linux installation. You should now be able to move on to the section, "Testing Your Tomcat Installation."

Testing Your Tomcat Installation

To test the Tomcat installation, you need to first start the Tomcat server. Table 1-5 contains the `startup` and `shutdown` commands for both operating systems.

Table 1-5. Tomcat Startup/Shutdown Commands

OS	STARTUP	SHUTDOWN
Windows NT/2000	TOMCAT_HOME\bin\startup.bat	TOMCAT_HOME\bin\shutdown.bat
Linux	TOMCAT_HOME /bin/startup.sh	TOMCAT_HOME /bin/shutdown.sh

NOTE *If you have installed Tomcat on Windows, a folder was placed in your Windows "Start" menu with shortcuts that allow you to start and stop your Tomcat server from there.*

Once Tomcat has started, open your browser to the following URL:

```
http://localhost:8080/
```

You should see a page similar to that shown in Figure 1-7.

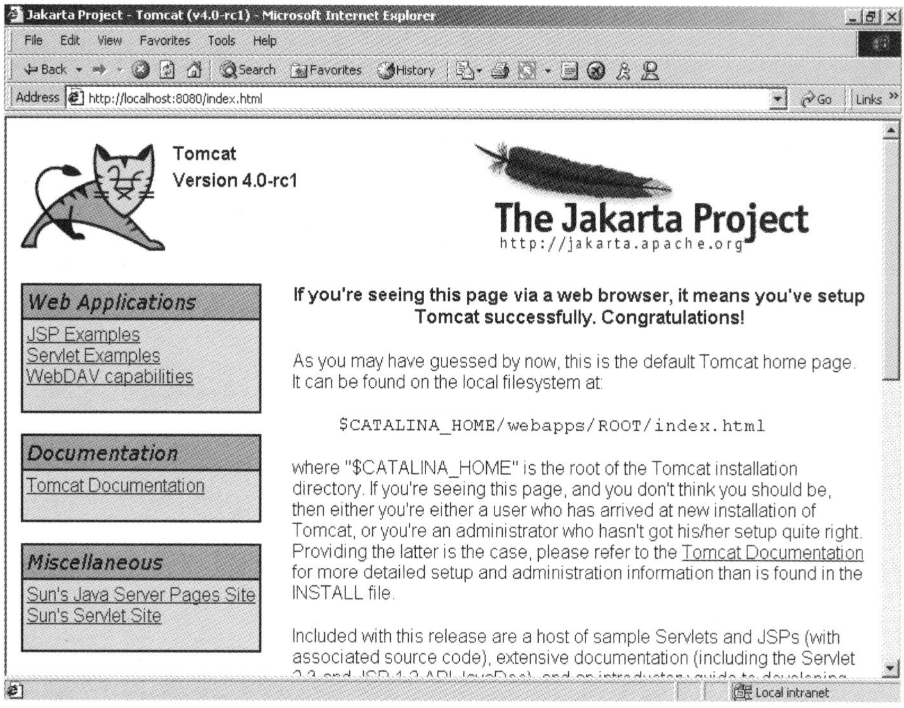

Figure 1-7. The Tomcat default page

If you would like to have all requests serviced on the default HTTP port of 80 instead of port 8080, you need to make the following change to the `TOMCAT_HOME/conf/server.xml` file and restart Tomcat:

From:

```
<!-- Define a non-SSL HTTP/1.1 Connector on port 8080 -->
  <Connector className="org.apache.catalina.connector.http.HttpConnector"
  port="8080" minProcessors="5" maxProcessors="75"
  acceptCount="10" debug="0"/>
```

To:

```
    <!-- Define a non-SSL HTTP/1.1 Connector on port 80 -->
  <Connector className="org.apache.catalina.connector.http.HttpConnector"
  port="80" minProcessors="5" maxProcessors="75"
  acceptCount="10" debug="0"/>
```

Now you should be able to open your browser to the following URL and see results similar to those shown in Figure 1-8:

```
http://localhost
```

The next step is to verify the installation of your JDK. You do this by executing one of the JSP examples provided with the Tomcat server. To execute an example JSP, start from the page shown in Figure 1-7 and choose JSP Examples. You should see a page similar to that shown in Figure 1-8.

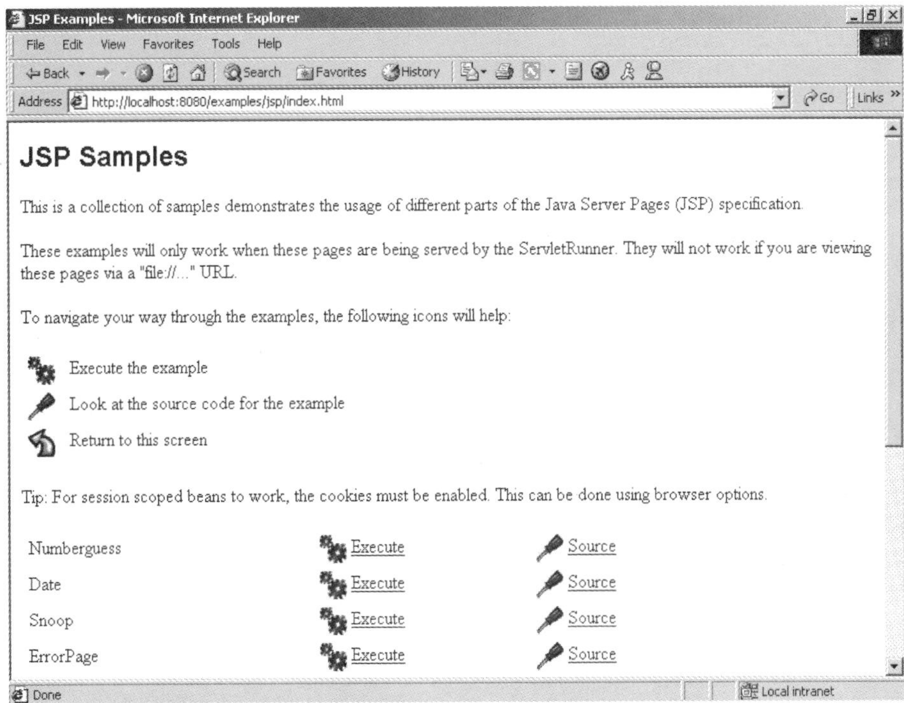

Figure 1-8. The JSP examples page

Now choose the JSP example Date and select the Execute link. If everything was installed properly, you should see a page similar to Figure 1-9 (with a different date, of course).

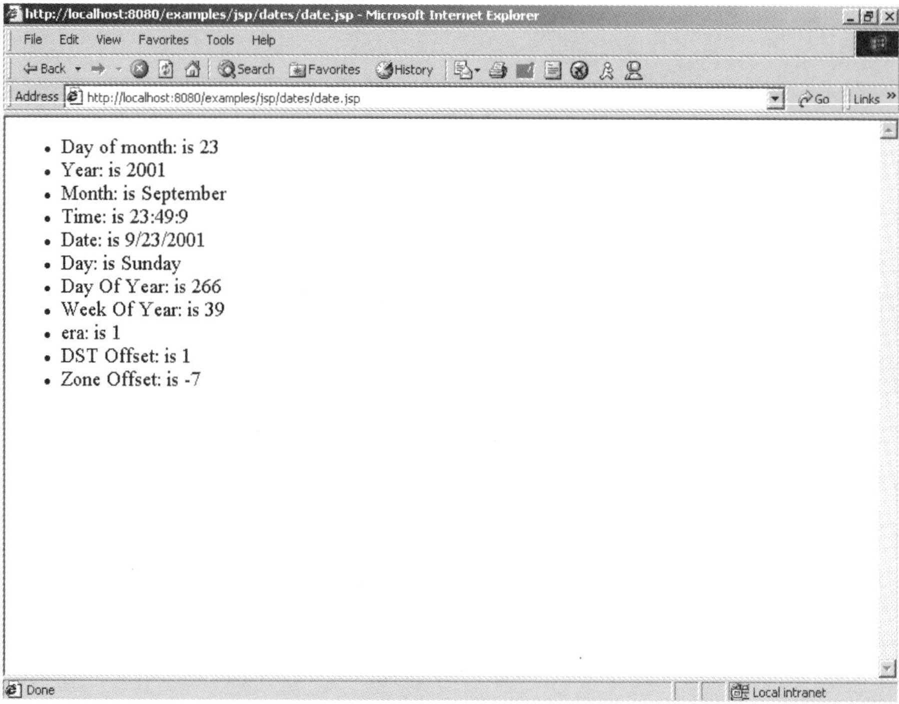

Figure 1-9. The JSP date page

If you do not see the previous page, make sure that the location of your `JAVA_HOME` environment variable matches the location of your JDK installation.

Summary

In this chapter, we introduced the Jakarta Tomcat server and discussed its main uses. We briefly discussed Java Web applications, which are at the core of the Tomcat server. We went on to install and configure Tomcat on both Windows NT/2000 and Linux. We also discussed some simple steps to test your new installation. In the next chapter, "Deploying Web Applications to Tomcat," we begin our discussions on how to create and deploy real Web applications using the Tomcat server.

CHAPTER 2

Deploying Web Applications to Tomcat

IN THIS CHAPTER, we

- Describe the Tomcat directory structure
- Manually deploy Web applications to Tomcat

Now that Tomcat is installed and running, let's look at the steps necessary to deploy a Web application. However, to do this we need to first examine the directory structure of Tomcat and then move on to actually deploying a Web application.

The Tomcat Directory Structure

Before you can start creating your own Web applications, you need to be familiar with the Tomcat directory structure. Table 2-1 describes the directories that compose a Tomcat installation. It is assumed that each of these directories is prepended with `TOMCAT_HOME`.

NOTE *As of this writing, Tomcat 4.0 is in beta. Therefore, these directories could change without notice.*

Table 2-1. The Tomcat Directory Structure

DIRECTORY	CONTAINS
/bin	Contains the startup and shutdown scripts for both Windows and Linux
/conf	Contains main configuration files for Tomcat. The two most important are `server.xml` and the global `web.xml`.
/server	Contains the Tomcat Java Archive files
/lib	Contains JAR files that the servlet engine is dependant upon
/common/lib	Contains the JAR files that are shared between Tomcat components
/jasper	Contains the JAR files that the JSP compiler, Jasper, depends upon
/logs	Contains Tomcat's log files
/src	Contains the source code used by the Tomcat server. Once Tomcat is released, it will probably contain only interfaces and abstract classes.
/webapps	The directory where all Web applications are deployed, and where you place your WAR file, when it is ready for deployment
/work	The directory where Tomcat places all servlets that are generated from JSPs. If you want to see exactly how a particular JSP is interpreted, look in this directory.

Just look over these directories for now because we examine most of these in detail in subsequent chapters. The directory that we are most interested in is `/webapps`, where all Web applications are deployed.

Manually Deploying Web Applications to Tomcat

In this section we cover the manual deployment of Web applications using Tomcat, and we are performing a manual deployment to fully explain the steps involved when deploying a Web application. In Chapter 5, we cover the deployment process using some of Tomcat's built-in functionality.

The best way to describe the deployment process is to create a Web application of our own that includes the major components that are found in most Java Web applications and then package it for deployment. The following sections walk you through all of the steps involved in manually deploying a Web application. The name of our Web application is `/apress`.

Creating the Web Application Directory Structure

The first thing you need to create when building a new Web application is the directory structure that will contain the application. The following list contains the directories that you must create to contain the /apress web application. Each one of these directories must be appended to the <TOMCAT_HOME>/webapps/ directory.

- /apress
- /apress/WEB-INF
- /apress/WEB-INF/classes
- /apress/WEB-INF/lib

NOTE *The name of our Web application,* /apress, *is the root of our directory structure.*

While the Web application is in development, I suggest creating the directory directly in the Tomcat /webapps directory. When the application is ready for deployment, you should package it into a WAR file and go through the production deployment process. We cover the production deployment process in the final section of this chapter ("Creating and Deploying a WAR File").

The last step in creating the Web application directory structure is adding a deployment descriptor. At this point, you will be creating a default web.xml file that contains only the DTD, describing the web.xml file, and an empty <webapp/> element. Listing 2-1 contains the source code for a default web.xml file.

Listing 2-1. The Source Code for a Default web.xml *File*

```
<?xml version="1.0" encoding="ISO-8859-1"?>

<!DOCTYPE web-app
    PUBLIC "-//Sun Microsystems, Inc.//DTD Web Application 2.3//EN"
    "http://java.sun.com/j2ee/dtds/web-app_2_3.dtd">

<web-app>
</web-app>
```

Now copy this file to the /apress/WEB-INF/ directory, and we will begin adding Web application components to it in the following sections.

Creating a Web Application ServletContext

After you have created the Web application directory structure, you must add a new ServletContext. The ServletContext defines a set of methods that components of a Web application use to communicate with the servlet container. The ServletContext acts as a container for the Web application, and there is only one ServletContext per Web application. We discuss the relationship between a ServletContext and its Web application in much more detail in Chapter 4.

To add a new ServletContext to Tomcat, you need to add the following entry to the TOMCAT_HOME/conf/server.xml file, setting the values for the path and docBase equal to the name of your Web application. This entry should be added inside the <Host> element, with the name localhost. Notice again that we are using apress as the name.

```
<Context path="/apress" docBase="apress" debug="0"
reloadable="true" />
```

We need to focus upon two elements in this entry. This first, path="/apress", tells the servlet container that all requests with /apress appended to the server's URL belong to the apress Web application. The second element, docBase="apress", tells the servlet container that the Web application exists in the Web application directory apress.

Adding JSPs

Now that you have added the Web application directory and ServletContext, you can start adding some server-side Java components. The first components we are going to add are a couple of JSPs.

The first of these JSPs displays a simple login screen containing a form with a username and password, which are passed on the HTTP request to the named action. Listing 2-1 contains the source code for the login.jsp page.

Listing 2-2. The Source Code for login.jsp

```
<html>
<head>
  <title>Apress Demo</title>
  <meta http-equiv="Content-Type" content="text/html; charset=iso-8859-1">
</head>
```

```
<body bgcolor="#FFFFFF" onLoad="document.loginForm.username.focus()">

  <table width="500" border="0" cellspacing="0" cellpadding="0">
    <tr>
      <td> </td>
    </tr>
    <tr>
    <td>
      <img src="/apress/images/monitor2.gif"></td>
    </tr>
    <tr>
      <td> </td>
    </tr>
  </table>
  <table width="500" border="0" cellspacing="0" cellpadding="0">
    <tr>
      <td>
        <table width="500" border="0" cellspacing="0" cellpadding="0">
          <form name="loginForm" method="post" action="servlet/chapter2.login">
          <tr>
            <td width="401"><div align="right">User Name: </div></td>
            <td width="399"><input type="text" name="username"></td>
          </tr>
          <tr>
            <td width="401"><div align="right">Password: </div></td>
            <td width="399"><input type="password" name="password"></td>
          </tr>
          <tr>
            <td width="401"> </td>
            <td width="399"><br><input type="Submit" name="Submit"></td>
          </tr>
          </form>
        </table>
      </td>
    </tr>
  </table>
</body>
</html>
```

As you look over this JSP, you can see that there is nothing special about it. The only thing that you should really pay attention to is the `action` of the form. It references a servlet in the package `chapter2` named `login`. This servlet, discussed in the next section ("Adding Servlets"), retrieves the `username/password` parameters from the request and performs its own processing.

There really is no process to Deploying a JSP: you simply need to copy it to the public directory of your Web application, which is `TOMCAT_HOME/webapps/apress/`, and the images that are referenced should be placed in an `images` directory that you have created in the `/apress` directory.

NOTE *The source code and images for all the examples in this text can be found at* `http://www.virtuas.com/publications.html`.

To see the results of this JSP, direct your browser to

```
http://localhost:8080/apress/login.jsp
```

If you changed your default HTTP port, as mentioned in Chapter 1, you need to reference the new port value. If everything was configured correctly, you should see an image similar to that shown in Figure 2-1.

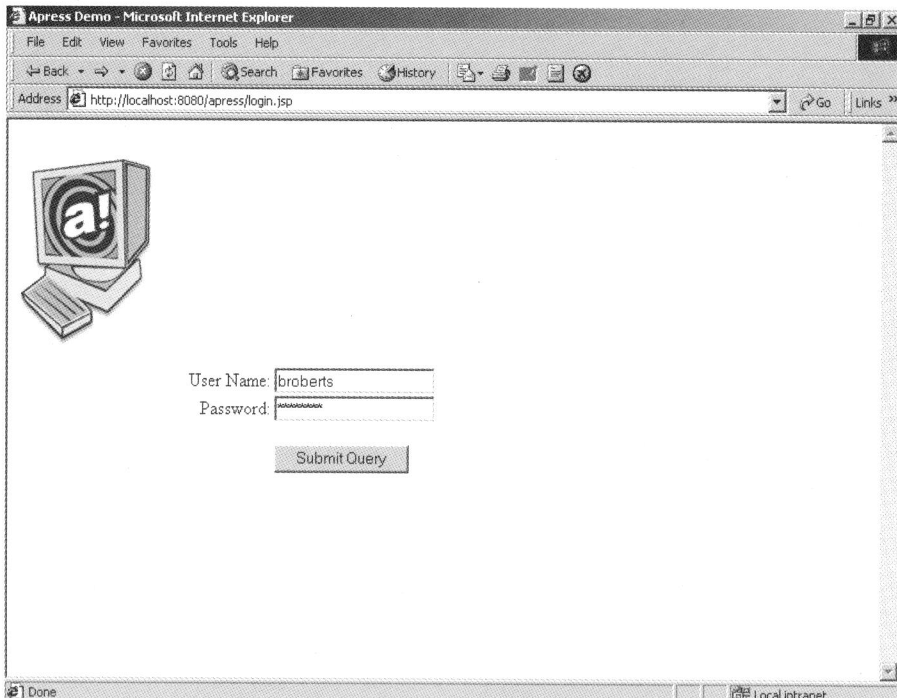

Figure 2-1. The ouput of the `login.jsp`

If you do not see a page similar to Figure 2-1, make sure you have the correct entry in the `server.xml` file, as described in the section, "Creating a Web Application `ServletContext`".

The second JSP you are adding is the target JSP referenced by the servlet defined in the following section "Adding Servlets". This JSP retrieves the request attribute `USER` that was added to the `request` by the servlet shown in Listing 2-4 of the following section. It then outputs the `String` value of the attribute. Listing 2-3 contains the source code for the target JSP.

Listing 2-3. The Source Code for `welcome.jsp`

```
<html>
<head>
  <title>Apress Demo</title>
  <meta http-equiv="Content-Type" content="text/html; charset=iso-8859-1">
</head>

  <table width="500" border="0" cellspacing="0" cellpadding="0">
    <tr>
      <td> </td>
    </tr>
    <tr>
    <td>
      <img src="/apress/images/monitor2.gif"></td>
    <td>
      <b>Welcome : <%= request.getAttribute("USER") %></b>
    </td>
    </tr>
    <tr>
      <td> </td>
    </tr>
  </table>
</body>
</html>
```

As we stated earlier, all you need to do to deploy this JSP is simply copy it to the public directory of your Web application, which in this case is `TOMCAT_HOME/webapps/apress/`.

Adding Servlets

The next component you are adding is a servlet, and this servlet will be the action of the `login.jsp`'s form. It retrieves the `username` and `password` values from the `HttpServletRequest`, looks up the real name of the associated user and then forwards the request to a target JSP. The source code for this servlet is shown in Listing 2-4.

NOTE *The value of the* `USER` *is static. Normally, you would perform a real lookup of some sort, but, for simplicity's sake, I am just returning the* `String Bob`.

Listing 2-4. The Source Code for `chapter2.login.java`

```
package chapter2

import javax.servlet.*;
import javax.servlet.http.*;
import java.io.*;
import java.util.*;

public class login extends HttpServlet {

  private String target = "/welcome.jsp";

  private String getUser(String username, String password) {

    // Just return a statice name
    // If this was reality, we would perform a SQL lookup
    return "Bob";
  }


  public void doGet(HttpServletRequest request,
    HttpServletResponse response)
    throws ServletException, IOException {

    // If it is a get request forward to doPost()
    doPost(request, response);
  }
```

```
  public void doPost(HttpServletRequest request,
    HttpServletResponse response)
    throws ServletException, IOException {

    // Get the username from the request
    String username = request.getParameter("username");
    // Get the password from the request
    String password = request.getParameter("password");

    String user = getUser(username, password);

    // Add the fake user to the request
    request.setAttribute("USER", user);

    // Forward the request to the target named
    ServletContext context = getServletContext();

    RequestDispatcher dispatcher =
      context.getRequestDispatcher(target);
    dispatcher.forward(request, response);
  }

}
```

To deploy a servlet to a Web application, you need to first compile the servlet and move it into the Web application's `/WEB-INF/classes` directory. For this example, you should compile this servlet and move it to the `/apress/WEB-INF/classes/chapter2/` directory.

NOTE *This class file is in the subdirectory* `chapter2` *because of its package name.*

The next step in deploying the `login` servlet is to add a servlet entry into the Web application's `web.xml` file.

NOTE *It is not necessary to add all servlets to the* `web.xml` *file. It is necessary only when the servlet requires additional information, such as initialization parameters.*

An example <servlet> element can be found in the following code snippet:

Example *<servlet>* Element

```
<servlet>
    <servlet-name>ExampleServlet</servlet-name>
    <servlet-class>packagename.ExampleServlet</servlet-class>
    <init-param>
      <param-name>parameter</param-name>
      <param-value>value</param-value>
    </init-param>
    <load-on-startup>1</load-on-startup>
</servlet>
```

This servlet entry contains a simple servlet definition. A description of each of its sub-elements can be found in Table 2-3.

Table 2-3 The Sub-Elements of a <servlet>

SUB-ELEMENT	DESCRIPTION
<servlet-name>	The canonical name for the deployed servlet
<servlet-class>	References the fully qualified class name of the servlet
<init-param>	An optional parameter containing a name/value pair that is passed to the servlet on initialization. It contains two sub-elements, <param-name> and <param-value>, which contain the name and value, respectively, to be passed to the servlet.
<load-on-startup>	Indicates the order in which each servlet should be loaded. Lower positive values are loaded first. If the value is negative or unspecified, the container can load the servlet at any time during startup.

To add our login servlet, we need to make the following entry into the TOMCAT_ROOT/apress/WEB-INF/web.xml file inside the <web-app></web-app> tag:

```
<servlet>
    <servlet-name>login</servlet-name>
    <servlet-class>chapter2.login</servlet-class>
</servlet>
```

That is all there is to it. To see your Web application in action, restart the Tomcat server and point your browser to:

```
http://localhost:8080/apress/login.jsp
```

You should see an image similar to that shown in the earlier Figure 2-1. Now enter a username and password and click on the "Submit Query" button. If everything went according to plan, you should see an image similar to that shown in Figure 2-2.

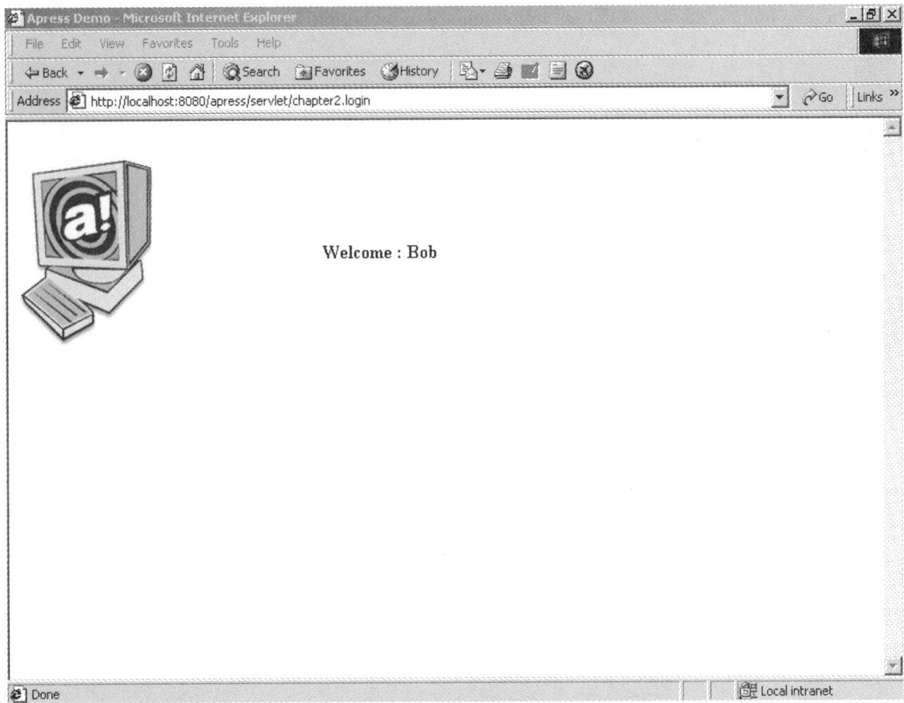

Figure 2-2. The `welcome.jsp` *page containing the HTML login form*

If you did not see an image similar to Figure 2-2, make sure that you have the servlet class in the appropriate directory and that your entry in the `web.xml` file matches the code snippet shown previously.

Adding Tag Libraries

The final component that we are adding to our Web application is a tag library. This library contains a single tag (HelloTag) that replaces every occurrence of the text <apress:hello/> with the literal string Hello. Although this is a silly example of a tag library, it does serve as a practical example of deploying a tag library. I am including a packaged JAR file containing this library, but, if you would like to create this yourself, the source code can be found in Listing 2-5 and 2-6.

Listing 2-5. The Source Code for HelloTag.java *Containing the Hello Tag Handler*

```
package chapter2

import javax.servlet.jsp.JspException;
import javax.servlet.jsp.JspTagException;
import javax.servlet.jsp.tagext.TagSupport;

public class HelloTag extends TagSupport
{
    public void HelloTag() {

    }

    // Method called when the closing hello tag is encountered
    public int doEndTag() throws JspException {

        try {

            // We use the pageContext to get a Writer
            // We then print the text string Hello
            pageContext.getOut().print("Hello");
        }
        catch (Exception e) {

            throw new JspTagException(e.getMessage());
        }
        // We want to return SKIP_BODY because this Tag does not support
        // a Tag Body
        return SKIP_BODY;
    }

    public void release() {
```

```
        // Call the parent's release to release any resources
        // used by the parent tag.
        // This is just good practice for when you start creating
        // hierarchies of tags.
        super.release();
    }
}
```

Listing 2-6. The Source Code for `taglib.tld`*, Including the Definition of the* `hello` *Tag.*

```
<?xml version="1.0" encoding="ISO-8859-1" ?>
<!DOCTYPE taglib
        PUBLIC "-//Sun Microsystems, Inc.//DTD JSP Tag Library 1.1//EN"
   "http://java.sun.com/j2ee/dtds/web-jsptaglibrary_1_1.dtd">

<!-- a tag library descriptor -->

<taglib>
  <tlibversion>1.0</tlibversion>
  <jspversion>1.1</jspversion>
  <shortname>apress</shortname>
  <uri>/apress</uri>

  <tag>
    <name>hello</name>
    <tagclass>chapter2.HelloTag</tagclass>
    <bodycontent>empty</bodycontent>
    <info>Just Says Hello</info>
  </tag>
</taglib>
```

To deploy this tag library, we need to make an entry to the `web.xml` file. The modified `web.xml` file can be found in Listing 2-7.

Listing 2-7. The Modified `web.xml` *Containing the Addition of our Tag Library*

```
<?xml version="1.0" encoding="ISO-8859-1"?>

<!DOCTYPE web-app PUBLIC
  '-//Sun Microsystems, Inc.//DTD Web Application 2.3//EN'
  'http://java.sun.com/j2ee/dtds/web-app_2_3.dtd'>
```

```
<web-app>
  <servlet>
    <servlet-name>login</servlet-name>
    <servlet-class>chapter2.login</servlet-class>
  </servlet>
  <taglib>
    <taglib-uri>/apress</taglib-uri>
    <taglib-location>/WEB-INF/lib/apress.jar</taglib-location>
  </taglib>
</web-app>
```

This `<taglib>` entry contains two sub-elements: `<taglib-uri>` and `<taglib-location>`. The `<taglib-uri>` sub-element tells the container how the tag library is to be referenced. For this example, we use the value `/apress`, which is how we will reference the tag library in our JSPs.

The second `<taglib>` sub-element, `<taglib-location>`, defines the location of the tag library descriptor (TLD). The TLD defines the tags contained in the library and the handlers that process the defined tags. In this instance, we are leaving the `TLD` in the `apress.jar` file; therefore, the `<taglib-location>` sub-element references the JAR as opposed to the actual `TLD`.

To complete the deployment of your Web application, copy the `apress.jar` file, which contains the tag library, and the `taglib.tld` from Listing 2-6 into the `TOMCAT_ROOT/apress/WEB-INF/lib` directory.

To test your tag library, you need to modify the `welcome.jsp` page: replace the `Welcome` message with a reference to the `<apress:hello />` tag. You need to also add a `taglib` directive referencing the `taglib.tld` to the `welcome.jsp` file. The modified JSP is shown in Listing 2-8.

Listing 2-8. The Modified `welcome.jsp` *Page Containing the Reference to the* `hello` *Tag*

```
<%@ taglib uri="/apress" prefix="apress" %>
<html>
<head>
  <title>Apress Demo</title>
  <meta http-equiv="Content-Type" content="text/html; charset=iso-8859-1">
</head>

  <table width="500" border="0" cellspacing="0" cellpadding="0">
    <tr>
      <td> </td>
    </tr>
```

```
      <tr>
      <td>
        <img src="/apress/images/monitor2.gif"></td>
      <td>
        <b><apress:hello /> : <%= request.getAttribute("USER") %></b>
      </td>
      </tr>
      <tr>
        <td> </td>
      </tr>
    </table>
  </body>
</html>
```

Now open the `login.jsp` page as described previously and run through the demo again. This time, instead of `Welcome : Bob`, you should see the message `Hello : Bob`.

Creating and Deploying a WAR File

When your Web application is ready for deployment, you need to package it for distribution. As we discussed in Chapter 1, Web applications are packaged in WAR files. To complete the chapter, we are going to "WAR up" your `/apress` Web application and deploy it. The steps are listed below:

1. Change to the root directory of your Web application. (In this case, the root directory is `TOMCAT_HOME/webapps/apress/`.)

2. Archive the Web application using the following command:

```
jar cvf apress.war .
```

3. Copy the resulting WAR file, `apress.war`, to the `TOMCAT_HOME/webapps` directory.

NOTE *If your are deploying this WAR file to the Tomcat installation that you were developing in, then you need to back-up your* `/apress` *development directory and remove it from the* `TOMCAT_HOME/webapps` *directory.*

4. If you haven't already, add a new `Context` entry to the `/TOMCAT_HOME/conf/server.xml` file, referencing the `apress` Web application.

5. Restart Tomcat.

Your application should now be running. If it isn't, check your entry into the `TOMCAT_HOME/conf/server.xml` file.

Summary

We covered a lot of information in this chapter. We described the Tomcat directory structure and then went on to describe the process of deploying JSPs, servlets, and tag libraries. We closed by archiving our `/apress` Web application and deploying it to Tomcat.

The next chapter continues our coverage of Web applications with a discussion of how Web applications are related to the `ServletContext`. These discussions include sample servlets and JSPs that demonstrate how the Web application affects `ServletContext`.

CHAPTER 3

Servlets, JSPs, and the *ServletContext*

IN THIS CHAPTER, we

- Describe the Java servlet architecture
- Describe the JavaServer pages architecture
- Define the `ServletContext` and its relationship to Web applications

In this chapter, we briefly discuss the Web application components that are hosted by the Tomcat container. We begin by discussing the Java servlet architecture. We then move on to describing JavaServer pages and conclude this chapter with a look at one of the most important characteristics of Web applications: the relationship between a Web application and its `ServletContext`.

The purpose of this chapter is to provide an introduction to the Web components hosted by the Tomcat container, namely servlets and JSPs. However, this chapter does not discuss all areas surrounding these topics. If you would like to read more about these technologies, you can find it on the JavaSoft Web site (`http://java.sun.com/`). You can also purchase two of my other texts *Pure JSP* and *Developing Java Servlets*, both of which are published by Sams Computer Publishing.

What Are Java Servlets?

A Java servlet is a platform-independent Web application component that is hosted in a JSP/servlet container. Servlets communicate with Web clients using a request/response model managed by a JSP/servlet container. Figure 3-1 graphically depicts the execution of a Java servlet.

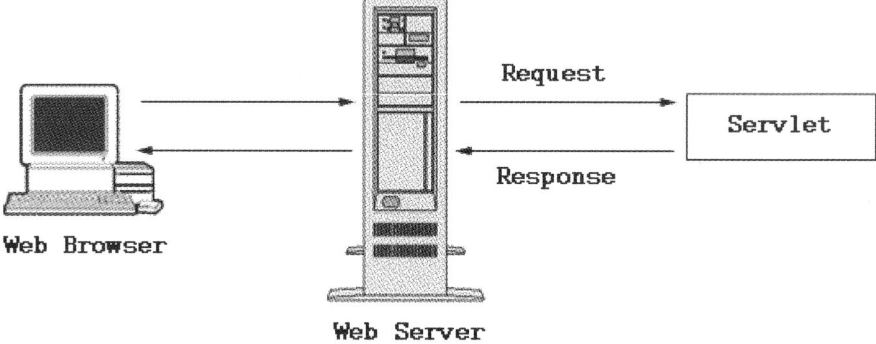

Figure 3-1. The Execution of a Java Servlet

The servlet architecture comprises two Java packages: `javax.servlet` and `javax.servlet.http`. The `javax.servlet` package contains the generic interfaces and classes that are implemented and extended by all servlets. The second package is the `java.servlet.http` package, which contains all the servlet classes that are specific to HTTP, such as a simple servlet that responds using HTML.

At the heart of this architecture is the interface `javax.servlet.Servlet`. The base class for all servlets, the `Servlet` interface defines five methods. The three most important of these methods and their functions are the `init()` method, which initializes a servlet; the `service()` method, which services client requests; and the `destroy()` method, which performs cleanup. These methods make up the servlet lifecycle methods. (We describe these lifecycle methods in a later section.)

All servlets must implement this interface, either directly or through inheritance. Figure 3-2 shows a simple object model that represents the servlet framework.

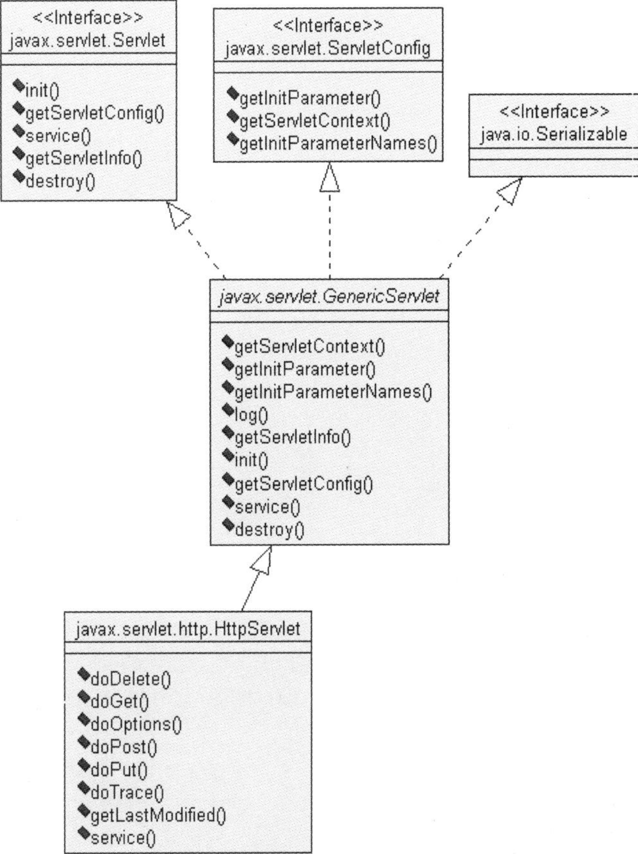

Figure 3-2. A simple object diagram of the servlet framework

The GenericServlet and HttpServlet Classes

The two main classes that extend the servlet architecture are the `GenericServlet` and `HttpServlet` classes. The `HttpServlet` class is extended from `GenericServlet`, which in turn implements the `Servlet` interface. When developing your own servlets, you'll most likely extend one of these two classes.

When extending the `GenericServlet` class, you must implement the `service()` method. The `GenericServlet.service()` method has been defined as an abstract method to force you to follow this framework. The `service()` method prototype is defined as follows:

```
public abstract void service(ServletRequest request,
  ServletResponse ressponse) throws ServletException, IOException;
```

The two parameters that are passed to the `service()` method are `ServletRequest` and `ServletResponse` objects. The `ServletRequest` object holds the information that is being sent to the servlet, and the `ServletResponse` object is where you place the data you want to send back to the client.

In contrast to the `GenericServlet`, when you extend `HttpServlet`, you don't usually implement the `service()` method. The `HttpServlet` class has already implemented the `service()` method for you. The following prototype contains the `HttpServlet.service()` method signature:

```
protected void service(HttpServletRequest request,
  HttpServletResponse response)
  throws ServletException, IOException;
```

When the `HttpServlet.service()` method is invoked, it reads the method type stored in the request and uses this value to determine which HTTP-specific methods to invoke. These are the methods that you want to override. If the method type is `GET`, it calls `doGet()`. If the method type is `POST`, it calls `doPost()`. Although the `service()` method has five other method types associated with it, we are focusing on the `doGet()` and `doPost()` methods.

You may have noticed the different request/response types in the `service()` method signature of the `HttpServlet` as opposed to the `GenericServlet` class. The `HttpServletRequest` and `HttpServletResponse` classes are just extensions of `ServletRequest` and `ServletResponse` with HTTP-specific information stored in them.

The Lifecycle of a Servlet

The lifecycle of a Java servlet follows a very logical sequence. The interface that declares the lifecycle methods is the `javax.servlet.Servlet` interface. These methods are the `init()`, the `service()`, and the `destroy()` methods. This sequence can be described in a simple three-step process:

1. A servlet is loaded and initialized using the `init()` method. This method is called when a servlet is preloaded or upon the first request to this servlet.

2. The servlet then services zero or more requests. The servlet services the request using the `service()` method.

3. The servlet is then destroyed and garbage-collected when the Web application containing the servlet shuts down. The method that is called upon shutdown is the `destroy()` method.

init()

The `init()` method is where the servlet begins its life. This method is called immediately after the servlet is instantiated, and it is called only once. The `init()` method should be used to create and initialize the resources that it will be using while handling requests. The `init()` method's signature is defined as follows:

```
public void init(ServletConfig config) throws ServletException;
```

The `init()` method takes a `ServletConfig` object as a parameter. This reference should be stored in a member variable so that it can be used later. A common way of doing this is to have the `init()` method call `super.init()` passing it the `ServletConfig` object.

The `init()` method also declares that it can throw a `ServletException`. If, for some reason, the servlet cannot initialize the resources necessary to handle requests, it should throw a `ServletException` with an error message that signifies the problem.

service()

The `service()` method services all requests received from a client using a simple request/response pattern. The `service()` method's signature is:

```
public void service(ServletRequest req, ServletResponse res)
  throws ServletException, IOException;
```

The `service()` method take two parameters, the first of which is a `ServletRequest` object that contains information about the service request, encapsulating information provided by the client. The `ServletResponse` object contains the information returned to the client.

You will not usually implement this method directly, unless you extend the `GenericServlet` abstract class. The most common implementation of the `service()` method is in the `HttpServlet` class. The `HttpServlet` class implements the servlet interface by extending `GenericServlet`. Its `service()` method supports standard HTTP/1.1 requests by determining the request type and calling the appropriate method.

destroy()

This method signifies the end of a servlet's life. When a Web application is shut down, the servlet's destroy() method is called. This is where all resources that were created in the init() method should be cleaned up. The signature of the destroy() can be found in the following code snippet:

```
public void destroy();
```

A Simple Servlet

Now that we have a basic understanding of what a servlet is and how it works, we are going to build a very simple servlet of our own. Its purpose is to service a request and respond by outputting the address of the client. After we have examined the source for this servlet, we'll take a look at the steps involved in compiling and installing it. Listing 3-1 contains the source code for this example.

Listing 3-1. The Source Code for our Simple Servlet SimpleServlet.java

```
package chapter3;

import javax.servlet.*;
import javax.servlet.http.*;
import java.io.*;
import java.util.*;

public class SimpleServlet extends HttpServlet {


  //Process the HTTP Get request
  public void doGet(HttpServletRequest request,
    HttpServletResponse response)
    throws ServletException, IOException {

    doPost(request, response);
  }

  //Process the HTTP Post request
  public void doPost(HttpServletRequest request,
    HttpServletResponse response)
    throws ServletException, IOException {
```

```
        response.setContentType("text/html");
        PrintWriter out = response.getWriter();

        out.println("<html>");
        out.println("<head><title>Simple Servlet</title></head>");
        out.println("<body>");

        // Outputs the address of the calling client
        out.println("Your address is " + request.getRemoteAddr()
          + "\n");

        out.println("</body></html>");
        out.close();
    }
}
```

NOTE *You will notice that the* SimpleServlet *does not implement the* init() *or* destroy() *methods. This is because it does not allocate or release resources in its processing. These methods can be ignored because the* GenericServlet *provides default implementations of these two methods.*

Now that you have had a chance to look over the SimpleServlet *source code, let's take a closer look at each of its integral parts. We will be examining where the servlet fits into the JSDK framework, the methods that the servlet implements, and the objects being used by the servlet. The following two methods are overridden in the* SimpleServlet*:*

- doGet()
- doPost()

Let's take a look at these two in more detail.

doGet() and doPost()

The SimpleServlet's doGet() and doPost() methods are where all of the business logic is truly performed, and, in this case, the doGet() method simply calls the doPost() method. The only time that the doGet() method is executed is when a get request is sent to the container. If a post request is received, the doPost() method services the request.

Both the doGet() and the doPost() receive HttpServletRequest and HttpServletResponse objects as parameters. The HttpServletRequest contains information sent from the client, and the HttpServletResponse contains the information that will be sent back to the client.

The first executed line of the doPost() method sets the content type of the response that is sent back to the client. This is done with the following code snippet:

```
response.setContentType("text/html");
```

This method sets the content type for the response. You can set this response property only once, and it must be set prior to writing to a Writer or an OutputStream. In our example, we are setting the response type to text/html.

The next thing we do is get a PrintWriter. This is accomplished by calling the ServletResponses's getWriter() method. The PrintWriter lets us write to the stream that is sent in the client response. Everything written to the PrintWriter is displayed in the client browser. This step is completed in the following line of code:

```
PrintWriter out = response.getWriter();
```

Once we have a reference to an object that allows you to write text back to the client, we use this object to write a message to the client. This message will include the HTML that formats this response for presentation in the client's browser. The next few lines of code show how this is done:

```
out.println("<html>");
out.println("<head><title>Simple Servlet</title></head>");
out.println("<body>");

// Outputs the address of the calling client
out.println("Your address is " + request.getRemoteAddr()
  + "\n");
```

The SimpleServlet uses a very clear-cut method of sending HTML to a client: it simply passes to the PrintWriter's println() method the HTML text that we want included in the response and closes the stream. The only thing that you may have a question about is the following few lines:

```
// Outputs the address of the calling client
out.println("Your address is " + request.getRemoteAddr()
  + "\n");
```

This section of code takes advantage of information sent by the client. It calls the HttpServletRequest's getRemoteAddr() method, which returns the address of the calling client. The HttpServletRequest object holds a great deal of HTTP-specific information about the client. If you would like to learn more about the HttpServletRequest or HttpServletResponse objects, you can find additional information at the following Sun Web site:

```
http://java.sun.com/products/servlet/
```

Building and Deploying the SimpleServlet

To see the SimpleServlet in action, we need to first create a Web application to host this servlet and then compile and deploy this servlet to the created Web application. These steps are described below:

1. Add the servlet.jar file to your CLASSPATH. This file should be in the <TOMCAT_HOME>/common/lib/ directory.

2. Compile the source for the SimpleServlet.

3. Copy the resulting class file to the <TOMCAT_HOME>webapps/apress/WEB-INF/classes/chapter3/ directory. The /chapter3 reference is appended because of the package name.

Once you have completed these steps, we can execute the SimpleServlet and see the results. Start Tomcat and open your browser to the following URL:

```
http://localhost:8080/apress/servlet/chapter3.SimpleServlet
```

You should see an image similar to that shown in Figure 3-3.

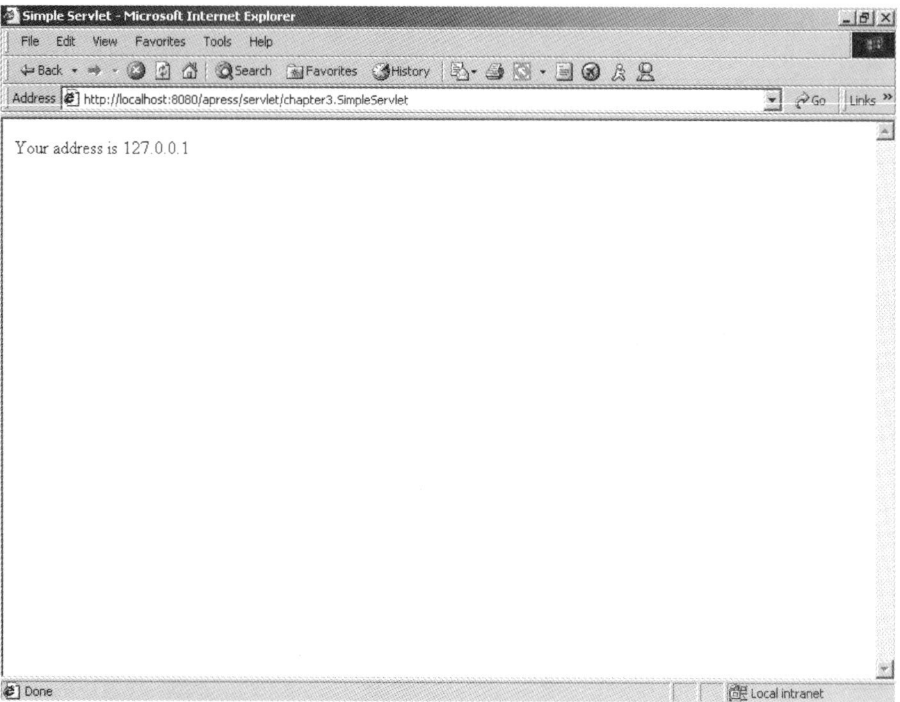

Figure 3-3. The output of `SimpleServlet`

NOTE *Notice that the URL to access* `SimpleServlet` *includes the string* `/servlet` *immediately preceding the reference to the actual servlet name. This text tells the container that you are referencing a servlet.*

What Are JavaServer Pages?

JavaServer pages, or JSPs, are a simple but powerful technology used most often to generate dynamic HTML on the server side. They are a direct extension of Java servlets with the purpose of allowing the developer to embed Java logic directly into a requested document. A JSP document must end with a `.jsp` extension. The following code snippet contains a simple example of a JSP file:

```
<HTML>
<BODY>

<% out.println("HELLO JSP READER"); %>
```

```
</BODY>
</HTML>
```

You can see that this document looks like any other HTML document with some added tags containing Java code. The source code is stored in a file called `hello.jsp` and copied to the document directory of the Web application that this JSP will be deployed to. When a request is made for this document, the server recognizes the `.jsp` extension and realizes that special handling is required. The JSP is then passed off to the JSP engine, which is just another servlet that is mapped to the extension `.jsp`, for processing.

The first time the file is requested, it is translated into a servlet and then compiled into an object that is loaded into resident memory. The JSP then services the request, and the output is sent back to the requesting client. On all subsequent requests, the server checks to see whether the original `.jsp` source file has changed. If it has not changed, the server invokes the previously compiled servlet object. If the source has changed, however, the JSP engine reparses the JSP source. Figure 3-4 illustrates these steps.

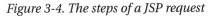

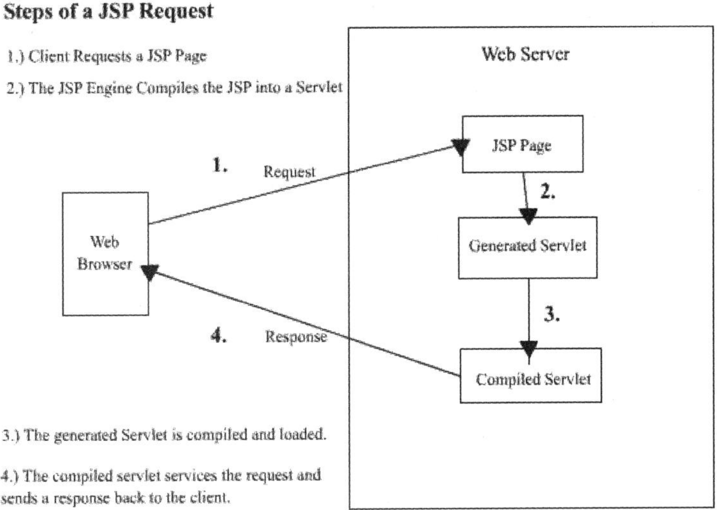
Steps of a JSP Request
1.) Client Requests a JSP Page
2.) The JSP Engine Compiles the JSP into a Servlet
Web Server
JSP Page
1.
Request
2.
Web Browser
Generated Servlet
3.
4.
Response
Compiled Servlet
3.) The generated Servlet is compiled and loaded.
4.) The compiled servlet services the request and sends a response back to the client.

Figure 3-4. The steps of a JSP request

NOTE *An essential point to remember about JSPs is that they are just servlets that are created from a combination of HTML and Java source. Therefore, they have the same resources and functionality of a servlet.*

The Components of a JavaServer Page

In this section, we are going to talk about the components of a JSP including directives, JSP scripting, implicit objects, and JSP standard actions. We describe each of these topics in the following sections.

JSP Directives

JSP directives are JSP elements that provide global information about a JSP page. An example would be a directive that included a list of Java classes to be imported into a JSP. The syntax of a JSP directive is as follows:

```
<%@ directive {attribute="value"} %>
```

Three possible directives are currently defined by the JSP specification: `page`, `include`, and `taglib`. Each of these directives is defined in the following sections.

The page Directive

The `page` directive defines information that globally affects the JavaServer page containing the directive. The syntax of a JSP directive is:

```
<%@ page {attribute="value"} %>
```

Table 3-1 defines the attributes for the `page` directive.

NOTE *Because all mandatory attributes are defaulted, the JSP developer is not required to specify any page directives.*

Table 3-1. The Attributes for the page *Directive*

ATTRIBUTE	DEFINITION
`language="scriptingLanguage"`	Tells the server which language will be used to compile the JSP file. (Java is currently the only available JSP language.)
`extends="className"`	Defines the parent class that the JSP will extend from
`import="importList"`	Defines the list of Java packages that will be imported into this JSP. It will be a comma-separated list of package names.
`session="true|false"`	Determines whether the session data will be available to this page. The default is true.
`buffer="none|size in kb"`	Determines whether the output stream is buffered. The default value is 8KB.
`autoFlush="true|false"`	Determines whether the output buffer will be flushed automatically, or whether it will throw an exception when the buffer is full. The default is true.
`isThreadSafe="true|false"`	Tells the JSP engine that this page can service multiple requests at one time. By default, this value is true. If this attribute is set to false, the `SingleThreadModel` is used.
`info="text"`	Represents information about the JSP page that can be accessed by invoking the page's `Servlet.getServletInfo()` method
`errorPage="error_url"`	Represents the relative URL to a JSP that will handle JSP exceptions
`isErrorPage="true|false"`	States whether or not the JSP is an errorPage. The default is false.
`contentType="ctinfo"`	Represents the MIME type and character set of the response sent to the client

An example page directive that imports the `java.util` package is included in the following code snippet:

```
<%@ page import="java.util.*" %>
```

The include Directive

The include directive is used to insert text and/or code at JSP translation time. The syntax of the include directive is shown in the following code snippet:

```
<%@ include file="relativeURLspec" %>
```

The file that the file attribute points to can reference a normal text HTML file or it can reference a JSP file, which is evaluated at translation time. This resource referenced by the file attribute must be local to the Web application that contains the include directive. An example include directive is:

```
<%@ include file="header.jsp" %>
```

NOTE *Because the* include *directive is evaluated at translation time, this included text is evaluated only once. This implies that, if the include resource changes, these changes are not reflected until the JSP/servlet container is restarted.*

The taglib Directive

The taglib directive states that the including page uses a custom tag library, uniquely identified by a URI and associated with a prefix that distinguishes each set of custom tags. The syntax of the taglib directive is as follows:

```
<%@ taglib uri="tagLibraryURI" prefix="tagPrefix" %>
```

The taglib attributes are described in Table 3-2.

Table 3-2. The Attributes for the taglib *Directive*

ATTRIBUTE	DEFINITION
uri	References a URI that uniquely names a custom tag library
prefix	Defines the prefix string used to distinguish a custom tag instance

JSP Scripting

Scripting is a JSP mechanism for directly embedding Java code fragments into an HTML page. Three scripting language components are involved in JSP scripting.

Each of these components has its appropriate location in the generated servlet. In this section, we look at each of these components.

Declarations

JSP declarations are used to define Java variables and methods in a JSP. A JSP declaration must be a complete declarative statement.

JSP declarations are initialized when the JSP page is first loaded. After the declarations have been initialized, they are available to other declarations, expressions, and scriptlets within the same JSP. The syntax for a JSP declaration is:

```
<%! declaration %>
```

A sample variable declaration using this syntax is declared here:

```
<%! String name = new String("BOB"); %>
```

A sample method declaration using the same syntax is declared here:

```
<%! public String getName() { return name; } %>
```

To get a better understanding of declarations, let's take the previous string declaration and actually embed it into a JSP document. The sample document would look similar to the following code snippet:

```
<HTML>
<BODY>

<%! String name = new String("BOB"); %>

</BODY>
</HTML>
```

When this document is initially loaded, the JSP code is converted to servlet code, and the name declaration is placed in the declaration section of the generated servlet. It is now available to all other components in the JSP.

Expressions

JSP expressions are JSP components whose text, upon evaluation by the container, is replaced with the resulting value of the container evaluation.

JSP expressions are evaluated at request time, with the result being inserted at the expression's referenced position in the `.jsp` file. If the resulting expression cannot be converted to a string, a translation time error occurs. If the conversion to a string cannot be detected during translation, a `ClassCastException` is thrown at request-time. The syntax of a JSP expression is:

```
<%= expression %>
```

A code snippet containing a JSP expression is shown here:

```
Hello <B><%= getName() %></B>
```

A sample JSP document containing a JSP expression is listed in the following code snippet:

```
<HTML>
<BODY>

<%! public String getName() { return "Bob"; } %>

Hello <B><%= getName() %></B>

</BODY>
</HTML>
```

Scriptlets

Scriptlets are the JSP components that bring all the JSP elements together. They can contain almost any coding statements that are valid for the language referenced in the language directive. They are executed at request time, and they can make use of all of the JSP components. The syntax for a scriptlet follows:

```
<% scriptlet source %>
```

With the first request of a JSP containing scripting code, the JSP is converted to servlet code and then compiled and loaded into resident memory. The actual source code, which is found between scriptlet tags `<% . . . %>`, is placed into the generated `service()` method that was created by the JSP compiler. The following code snippet contains a simple JSP that uses a scripting element to print the text "Hello Bob" to the requesting client:

```
<HTML>
<BODY>

<% out.println("Hello Bob"); %>

</BODY>
</HTML>
```

JSP Error Handling

All development methods need a robust mechanism for error handling, and the JSP architecture provides an error-handling solution through the use of JSPs that are written exclusively to handle JSP errors.

The errors that occur most are runtime errors that arise in either the body of the JSP page or in some other object that is called from the body of the JSP page. The request time errors that result in an exception being thrown can be caught and handled in the body of the calling JSP, which would signal the end of the error. The exceptions that are not handled in the calling JSP result in the forwarding of the client request, including the uncaught exception, to an error page specified by the offending JSP.

Creating a JSP Error Page

Creating a JSP error page is a very simple process. You simply need to create a basic JSP and then tell the JSP engine that the page is an error page. This is accomplished by setting the JSP's page directive attribute, `isErrorPage`, to true. Listing 3-2 contains the source code for a sample error page.

Listing 3-2. The Source Code of `errorpage.jsp`

```
<html>

<%@ page isErrorPage="true" %>

Bob there has been an error: <%= exception.getMessage() %> has been reported.

</body>
</html>
```

The first JSP-related line in this page tells the JSP compiler that this JSP is an error page. This code snippet is:

```
<%@ page isErrorPage="true" %>
```

The second JSP-related section uses the implicit exception object that is part of all JSP error pages to output the error message contained in the unhandled exception that was thrown in the offending JSP.

Using a JSP Error Page

To see how an error page works, let's create a simple JSP that throws an uncaught exception. The JSP found in Listing 3-3 uses the error page we previously created.

Listing 3-3. The Source Code of `testerror.jsp`

```
<%@ page errorPage="errorpage.jsp" %>

<%

  if ( true ) {

    // Just throw an exception
    throw new Exception("An uncaught Exception");
  }

%>
```

Notice in this listing that the first line of code sets the `errorPage` equal to `errorpage.jsp` (the name of our error page). To make your JSP aware of an error page, you simply need to add the `errorPage` attribute to the page directive and set its value equal to the location of your JSP error page. The rest of our example simply throws an exception that will not be caught. To see this example in action, copy both of these JSPs to the `<TOMCAT_HOME>/webapps/apress/` directory and open the `testerror.jsp` page in your browser. You will see a page similar to that shown in Figure 3-5.

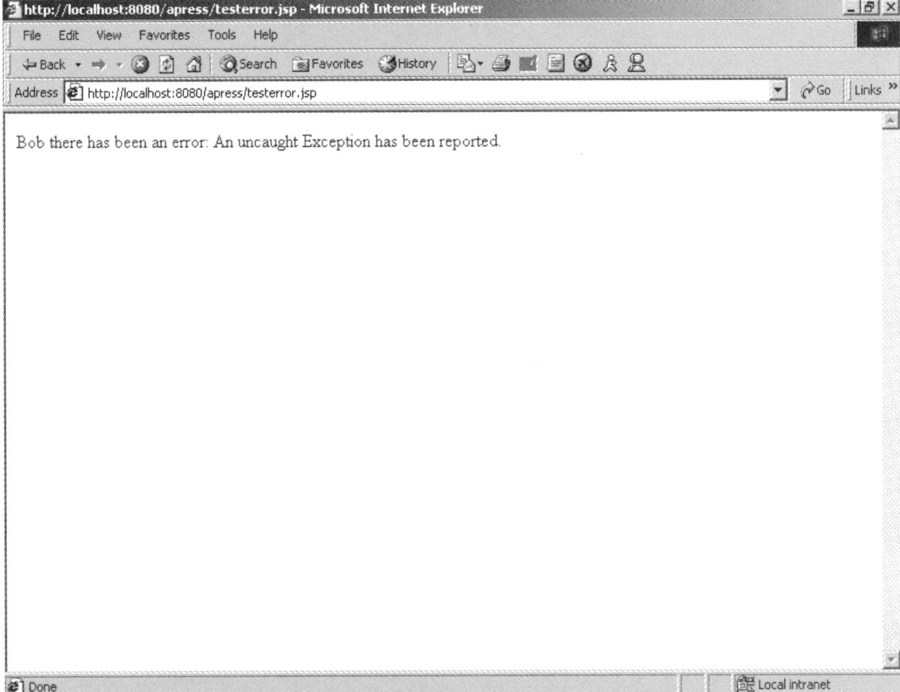

Figure 3-5. The output of the `testerror.jsp` *example*

Implicit Objects

As a JSP author, you have implicit access to certain objects that are available for use in all JSP documents. These objects are parsed by the JSP engine and inserted into the generated servlet as if you defined them yourself.

out

The implicit `out` object represents a `JspWriter`, which is derived from a `java.io.Writer`, that provides a stream back to the requesting client. The most common method of this object is the `out.println()` method, which prints text to be displayed in the client's browser. Listing 3-4 provides an example using the implicit out object.

Listing 3-4. The Source Code of `out.jsp`

```
<%@ page errorPage="errorpage.jsp" %>

<html>
```

```
  <head>
    <title>Use Out</title>
  </head>
  <body>
    <%
      // Print a simple message using the implicit out object.
      out.println("<center><b>Hello Bob!</b></center>");
    %>
  </body>
</html>
```

To execute this example, copy this file to the `<TOMCAT_HOME>/webapps/apress/` directory and then open your browser to the following URL:

```
http://localhost:8080/apress/out.jsp
```

You should see a page similar to that shown in Figure 3-6.

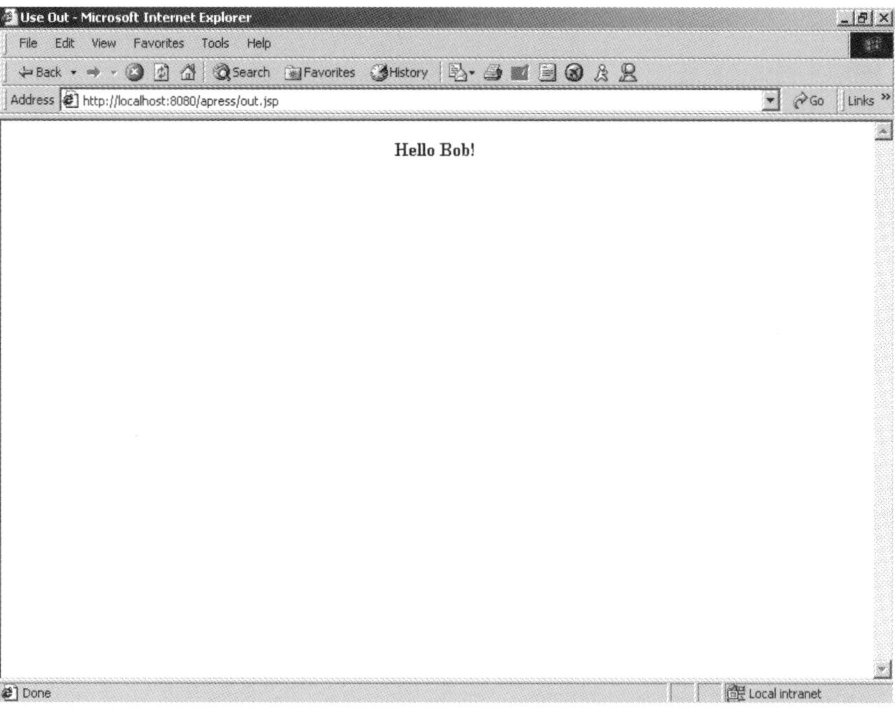

Figure 3-6. The output of `out.jsp`

request

The first of the implicit objects is the `request` object. This object represents the `javax.servlet.http.HttpServletRequest` interface, which we discussed earlier. The `request` object is associated with every HTTP request.

One of the more common uses for the request object is to access request parameters. You can do this by calling the request object's `getParameter()` method with the parameter name you are seeking. It returns a string with the value matching the named parameter. An example using the implicit request object can be found in Listing 3-5.

Listing 3-5. The Source Code of `request.jsp`

```
<%@ page errorPage="errorpage.jsp" %>

<html>
  <head>
    <title>UseRequest</title>
  </head>
  <body>
    <%
      out.println("<b>Welcome: " +
        request.getParameter("user") + "</b>");
    %>
  </body>
</html>
```

You can see that this JSP calls the `request.getParameter()` method passing in the parameter user. This looks for the key user in the parameter list and returns the value, if it is found. Enter the following URL into your browser to see the results from this page:

```
http://localhost:8080/apress/request.jsp?user=Bob
```

After loading this URL, you should see a page similar to that shown in Figure 3-7.

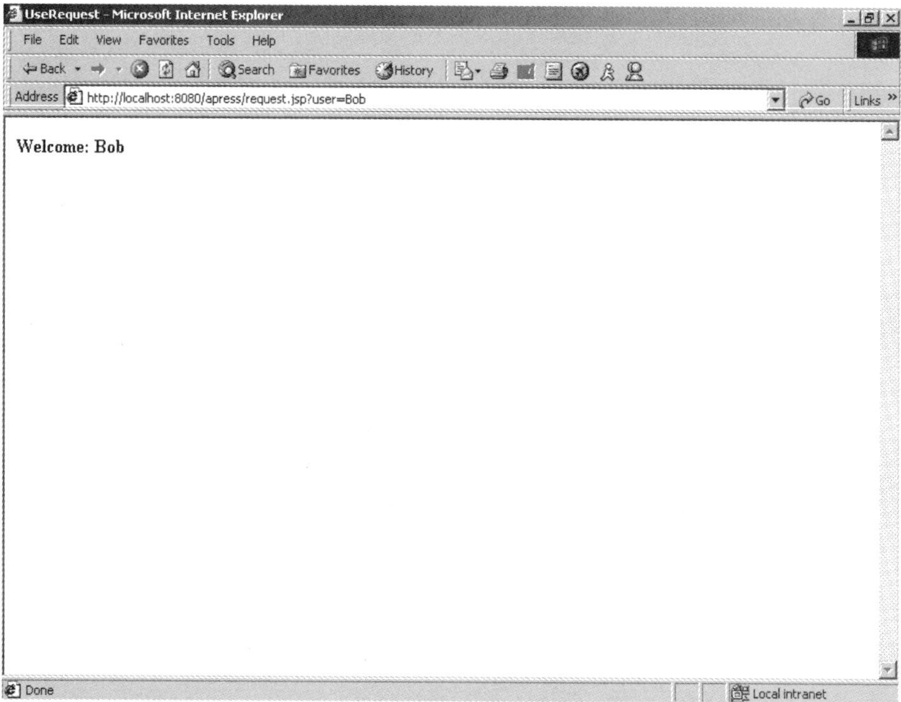

Figure 3-7. The output of `request.jsp`

response

The implicit `response` object represents the `javax.servlet.http.HttpServletResponse` object. The `response` object is used to pass data back to the requesting client. This implicit object provides you with all of the functionality of the `HttpServletRequest`, just as if you were executing in a servlet. One of the more common uses for the `response` object is writing HTML output back to the client browser; however, the JSP API already provides access to a stream back to the client using the implicit `out` object.

pageContext

The `pageContext` object provides access to the namespaces associated with a JSP. It also provides accessors to several other JSP implicit objects.

session

The implicit `session` object represents the `javax.servlet.http.HttpSession` object, which is used to store objects in between client requests providing an almost state-full HTTP interactivity. An example of using the session object is shown in Listing 3-6.

Listing 3-6. The Source Code of session.jsp

```
<%@ page errorPage="errorpage.jsp" %>

<html>
  <head>
    <title>Session Example</title>
  </head>
  <body>
    <%
      // get a reference to the current count from the session
      Integer count = (Integer)session.getAttribute("COUNT");

      if ( count == null ) {

        // If the count was not found create one
        count = new Integer(1);
        // and add it to the HttpSession
        session.setAttribute("COUNT", count);
      }
      else {

        // Otherwise increment the value
        count = new Integer(count.intValue() + 1);
        session.setAttribute("COUNT", count);
      }
      out.println("<b>This page has been accessed: "
        + count + " times.</b>");
    %>
  </body>
</html>
```

To use this example, copy the JSP to the <TOMCAT_HOME>webapps/apress/ directory and open your browser to the following URL:

```
http://localhost:8080/apress/session.jsp
```

If everything went well, you should see a page similar to Figure 3-8.

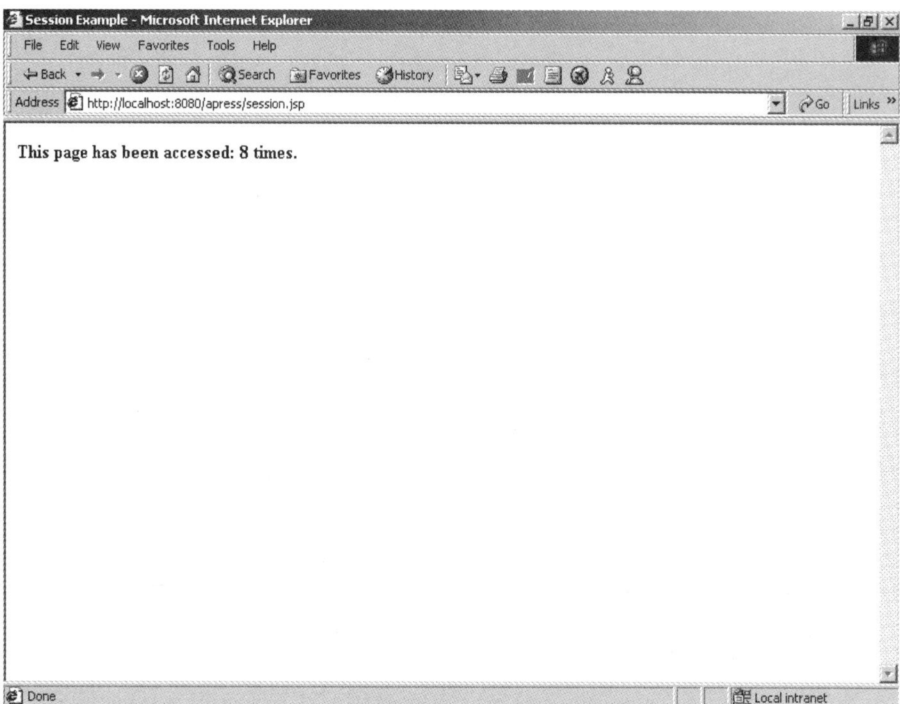

Figure 3-8. The output of `session.jsp`

Click on your reload button a few times to see the count increment.

application

The `application` object represents the `javax.servlet.ServletContext`, and it is most often used to access objects that are stored in the `ServletContext` to be shared between Web components. It is a great place to share objects between JSPs and servlets. In the following example, we use the application object to store and access our application's specific information. An example using the application object can be found later in this chapter.

config

The implicit `config` object holds a reference to the `ServletConfig`, which contains configuration information about the JSP/servlet engine containing the Web application in which this JSP resides.

page

The page object contains a reference to the current instance of the JSP being accessed. You use the page object just as you would a this object: to reference the current instance of the generated servlet representing this JSP.

exception

The implicit exception object provides access to an uncaught exception thrown by a JSP. It is only available in JSPs that have a page with the attribute isErrorPage set to true.

Standard Actions

JSP standard actions are predefined custom tags that can be used to easily encapsulate common actions. Six standard actions are available to JSP developers. Each group is defined and used in the following sections.

<jsp:useBean>

The first JavaBean standard action is <jsp:useBean>. This standard action creates or looks up an instance of a JavaBean with a given scope and ID. The <jsp:useBean> action is very flexible. When a <useBean> action is encountered, it tries to find an existing object using the same ID and scope. If it cannot find an existing instance, it attempts to create the object and store it in the named scope associated with the given ID. The syntax of the <jsp:useBean> action is defined as follows:

```
<jsp:useBean id="name"
        scope="page|request|session|application"
        typeSpec>
        body
</jsp:useBean>

typeSpec ::=class="className" |
        class="className" type="typeName" |
        type="typeName" class="className" |
        beanName="beanName" type="typeName" |
        type="typeName" beanName="beanName" |
        type="typeName"
```

Table 3-3 contains the attributes of the <jsp:useBean> action.

Table 3-3. The Attributes for the `<jsp:useBean>` *Action*

ATTRIBUTE	DEFINITION
id	Represents the key associated with the instance of the object in the specified scope. This key is case sensitive.
scope	Represents the life of the referenced object. The scope options are page, request, session, and application.
class	Represents the fully qualified class name that defines the implementation of the object. The class name is also case sensitive.
beanName	References the name of the JavaBean
type	Specifies the type of scripting variable defined. If this attribute is unspecified, the value is the same as the value of the class attribute.

<jsp:setProperty>

The second standard action related to using JavaBeans in JSPs is `<jsp:setProperty>`. This action sets the value of a bean's property. Its name attribute represents an object that must already be defined and in scope. The syntax for the `<jsp:setProperty>` action is:

```
<jsp:setProperty name="beanName" propexpr />
```

In the preceding syntax, the name attribute represents the name of the bean whose property you are setting, and `propexpr` can be represented in the following syntax:

```
property="*" |
property="propertyName" |
property="propertyName" param="parameterName" |
property="propertyName" value="propertyValue"
```

Table 3-4 contains the attributes and their descriptions for the `<jsp:setProperty>` action.

Table 3-4. The Attributes for the `<jsp:setProperty>` *Action*

ATTRIBUTE	DEFINITION
`name`	Represents the name of the bean instance defined by a `<jsp:useBean>` action or some other action
`property`	Represents the bean property for which you want to set a value. If you set `propertyName` to an asterisk (*),the action iterates over the current `ServletRequest` parameters, matching parameter names and value types to property names and setter method types, and setting each matched property to the value of the matching parameter. If a parameter has an empty string for a value, the corresponding property is left unmodified.
`param`	Represents the name of the request parameter whose value you want to set the named property to. A `<jsp:setProperty>` action cannot have both `param` and `value` attributes referenced in the same action.
`value`	Represents the value assigned to the named bean's property.

<jsp:getProperty>

The last standard action that relates to integrating JavaBeans into JSPs is `<jsp:getProperty>`. It takes the value of the referenced bean's instance property, converts it to a `java.lang.String`, and places it on the output stream. The referenced bean instance must be defined and in scope before this action is used. The syntax for the `<jsp:getProperty>` action is:

```
<jsp:getProperty name="name" property="propertyName" />
```

Table 3-5 contains the attributes and their descriptions for the `<jsp:getProperty>` action.

Table 3-5. The Attributes for the `<jsp:getProperty>` *Standard Action*

ATTRIBUTE	DEFINITION
`name`	Represents the name of the bean instance from which the property is obtained, defined by a `<jsp:useBean>` action or some other action
`property`	Represents the bean property for which you want to get a value

<jsp:param>

The `<jsp:param>` action is used to provide parameters and values to the JSP standard actions `<jsp:include>`, `<jsp:forward>`, and `<jsp:plugin>`. The syntax of the `<jsp:param>` action follows:

```
<jsp:param name="name" value="value"/>
```

Table 3-6 contains the attributes and their descriptions for the `<jsp:param>` action.

Table 3-6. The Attributes for the `<jsp:param>` *Action*

ATTRIBUTE	DEFINITION
name	Represents the name of the parameter being referenced
value	Represents the value of the named parameter

<jsp:include>

The `<jsp:include>` standard action provides a method for including additional static and dynamic Web components in a JSP. The syntax for this action is as follows:

```
<jsp:include page="urlSpec" flush="true">
    <jsp:param . . . />
</jsp:include>
```

Table 3-7 contains the attributes and their descriptions for the `<jsp:include>` action.

Table 3-7. The Attributes for the `<jsp:include>` *Action*

ATTRIBUTE	DEFINITION
page	Represents the relative URL of the resource to be included
flush	Represents a mandatory boolean value stating whether the buffer should be flushed

NOTE *It is important to note the difference between the* include *directive and the* include *standard action. The directive is evaluated only once, at translation time, whereas the standard action is evaluated with every request.*

This syntax description does a request-time inclusion of a URL that is passed an optional list of param sub-elements that are used to argument the request.

<jsp:forward>

The <jsp:forward> standard action enables the JSP engine to execute a run-time dispatch of the current request to another resource existing in the current Web application, including static resources, servlets, or JSPs. The appearance of <jsp:forward> effectively terminates the execution of the current JSP.

NOTE *A* <jsp:forward> *action can contain* <jsp:param> *subattributes. These subattributes act as parameters that are forwarded to the targeted resource.*

The syntax of the <jsp:forward> action is:

```
<jsp:forward page="relativeURL">
    <jsp:param . . ./>
</jsp:forward>
```

This action contains a single attribute, page, which represents the relative URL of the target of the forward.

<jsp:plugin>

The last standard action that we will discuss is the <jsp:plugin> action. This action enables a JSP author to generate the required HTML, using the appropriate client-browser independent constructs that result in the download and subsequent execution of the specified applet or JavaBeans component.

The <jsp:plugin> tag, once evaluated, is replaced by either an <object> or <embed> tag, as appropriate for the requesting user agent. The attributes of the <jsp:plugin> action provide configuration data for the presentation of the embedded element. The syntax of the <jsp:plugin> action is as follows:

```
<jsp:plugin type="pluginType"
    code="classFile"
    codebase="relativeURLpath">

    <jsp:params>

    </jsp:params>
</jsp:plugin>
```

Table 3-8 contains the attributes and their descriptions for the `<jsp:plugin>` action.

Table 3-8. The Attributes for the `<jsp:plugin>` *Action*

ATTRIBUTE	DEFINITION
`type`	Represents the type of plugin to include. An example of this would be an applet.
`code`	Represents the name of the class that the plugin will execute.
`codebase`	References the base or relative path of where the code attribute can be found

The `<jsp:plugin>` action also supports the use of the `<jsp:params>` tag to supply the plugin with parameters, if necessary.

The *ServletContext* and its Relationship to a Web Application

Before we can get started discussing the relationship between a Web application and its `ServletContext`, you need to know what a `ServletContext` is. A `ServletContext` is an object belonging to the `javax.servlet` package. It defines a set of methods that are used by server-side components of a Web application to communicate with the servlet container.

One of the more common uses of the `ServletContext` is as a storage area for objects that need to be available to all of the server-side components of a Web application. It is like a "shared memory" segment for Web applications. The objects stored in the `ServletContext` exist for the life of a Web application. Four `ServletContext` methods are used to provide this shared-memory functionality. Table 3-9 describes each of these methods.

Table 3-9. The ServletContext *"Shared Memory" Methods*

METHOD	DESCRIPTION
setAttribute(java.lang.String name, java.lang.Object object)	Binds an Object to a given attribute name and stores the Object in the current ServletContext. If the specified name is already in use, this method removes the old attribute binding and binds the name to the new Object.
getAttribute(java.lang.String name)	Returns the Object referenced by the given name, or null if there is no attribute bind to the given name
removeAttribute(java.lang.String name)	Removes the attribute with the given name from the ServletContext
getAttributeNames()	Returns an enumeration of strings containing the attribute names stored in the current ServletContext

For now, let's just take a quick look at these methods. We'll examine them in much more detail in the following sections.

The Relationship Between a Web Application and the ServletContext

In Chapter 2, "Deploying Web Applications to Tomcat," you added a new Context entry in the TOMCAT_HOME/conf/server.xml file. When you did this, you created a new Web application. With the addition of this Web application, you also created a new ServletContext. This is due to the relationship between a ServletContext and a Web application.

For every Web application there is a ServletContext, but only one instance of a ServletContext can be associated with each Web application. This relationship is required by the servlet specification and is enforced by all servlet containers.

In the rest of this chapter, we'll focus on this relationship of exclusivity because it is what ensures that there are no process or resource collisions between Web applications.

Examples of How the Web Application Affects Web Application Components

To see the relationship between the `ServletContext` and Web application in action, we'll use the `/apress` Web application from Chapter 2 and create another Web application named `/apress2`.

To add the second Web application, follow the steps described in the "Manually Deploying Web Applications to Tomcat" section in Chapter 2, substituting `/apress` with `/apress2`. Once this is complete, you will have two distinct Web applications deployed to Tomcat. Figure 3-9 depicts the relationship between your two Web applications.

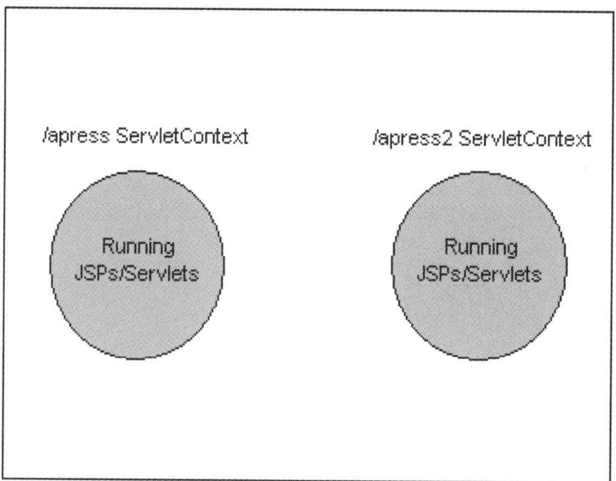

Figure 3-9. The relationship of `/apress` *and* `/apress2`

In each of these Web applications, we are going to deploy two Web components: a servlet and a JSP. The first, a simple servlet, doesn't perform any special kind of magic, but it does leverage the `ServletContext`. The source code for the servlet can be found in Listing 3-7.

Listing 3-7. The Souce Code of `chapter3.ContextTest.java`

```
package chapter3;

import javax.servlet.*;
```

```
import javax.servlet.http.*;
import java.io.*;
import java.util.*;

public class ContextTest extends HttpServlet {

  private static final String CONTENT_TYPE = "text/html";

  public void init() throws ServletException {

  }

  public void doGet(HttpServletRequest request,
    HttpServletResponse response)
    throws ServletException, IOException {

    doPost(request, response);
  }

  public void doPost(HttpServletRequest request,
    HttpServletResponse response)
    throws ServletException, IOException {

    // Get a reference to the ServletContext
    ServletContext context = getServletContext();
    // Try to get the count attribute from the ServletContext
    Integer count = (Integer)context.getAttribute("count");

    // If there was no attribute count, then create
    // one and add it to the ServletContext
    if ( count == null ) {

      count = new Integer(0);
      context.setAttribute("count", new Integer(0));
    }

    response.setContentType(CONTENT_TYPE);
    PrintWriter out = response.getWriter();
    out.println("<html>");
    out.println("<head><title>ContextTest</title></head>");
    out.println("<body>");
    // Output the current value of the attribute count
    out.println("<p>The current COUNT is : " + count + ".</p>");
```

```
            out.println("</body></html>");

            // Increment the value of the count attribute
            count = new Integer(count.intValue() + 1);
            // Add the new value of count to the ServletContext
            context.setAttribute("count", count);
        }

        public void destroy() {
        }
    }
```

As you look over this servlet, you notice that it performs the following steps:

1. It gets a reference to the `ServletContext` using the `getServletContext()` method.

```
ServletContext context = getServletContext();
```

2. Once it has a reference to the `ServletContext`, it tries to get the `count` attribute from the `ServletContext` using the `getAttribute()` method.

```
Integer count = (Integer)context.getAttribute("count");
```

3. It then checks to see if the attribute `count` existed in the `ServletContext`. If the attribute was not found, it is created and added to the `ServletContext` using the `setAttribute()` method.

```
if ( count == null ) {

    count = new Integer(0);
    context.setAttribute("count", new Integer(0));
}
```

4. If the attribute `count` was found, its value is printed to the output stream.

```
out.println("<p>The current COUNT is : " + count + ".</p>");
```

5. The attribute is then incremented and added back to the `ServletContext`.

```
count = new Integer(count.intValue() + 1);
context.setAttribute("count", count);
```

After you have looked over this servlet, you should compile it and move the class file into the `TOMCAT_HOME/webapps/apress/WEB-INF/classes/chapter3` and `TOMCAT_HOME/webapps/apress2/WEB-INF/classes/chapter3` directories. We won't execute this servlet until we have also deployed the following JSP.

Because the JSP that you will be using is much like the preceding servlet, we won't go through the steps again. Essentially the same actions are performed, but in a JSP. The source code for the JSP can be found in Listing 3-8.

Listing 3-8. The Source Code of `ContextTest.jsp`

```
<HTML>
<HEAD>
<TITLE>
ContextTest
</TITLE>
</HEAD>
<BODY>
<H1>
<%
  // Get the count attribute
  Integer count = (Integer)application.getAttribute("count");

  // If count is null, create a new Integer
  // and add it to the application/ServletContext
  if ( count == null ) {

    count = new Integer(0);
    application.setAttribute("count", count);
  }
%>

The current COUNT is : <%= count %>

<%
  // Increment the current count value
  // and add it to the ServletContext
  count = new Integer(count.intValue() + 1);
  application.setAttribute("count", count);
%>

</H1>
</BODY>
</HTML>
```

After you look over this JSP, copy it to both the `TOMCAT_HOME/webapps/apress/` and `TOMCAT_HOME/webapps/apress2/` directories.

Now that both Web components have been deployed to both of the Web applications, let's take a look at how being in separate Web applications actually affects these components. To begin our experiment, you need to open a Web browser to the following URL:

```
http://localhost:8080/apress/ContextTest.jsp
```

You should see a page similar to Figure 3-10, with a `count` value of `0`.

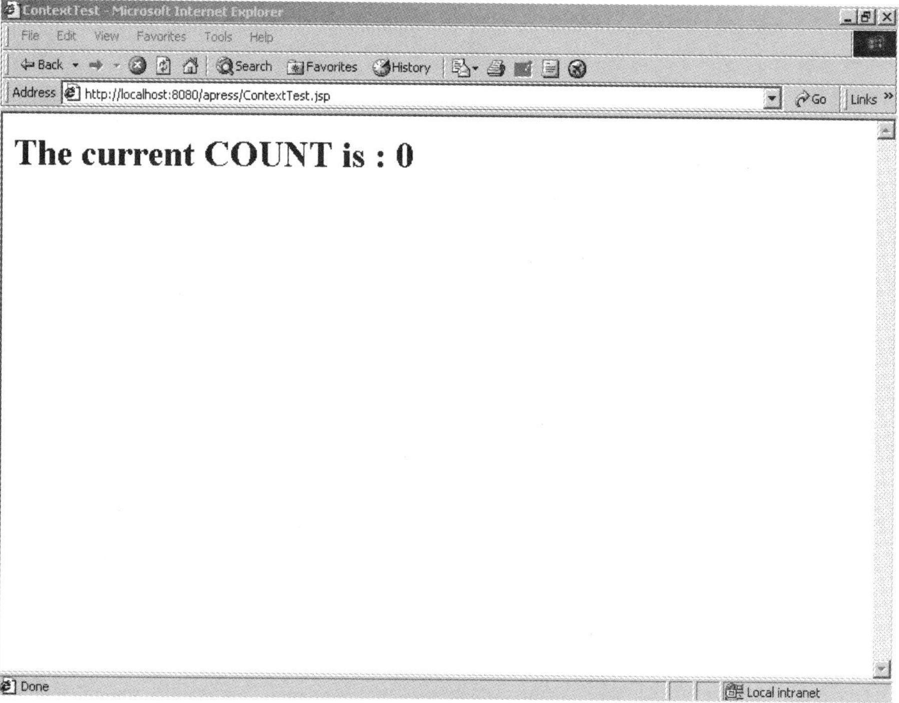

Figure 3-10. `ContextTest.jsp` *after initial load*

Go ahead and click on the Refresh button a few times. You should see the value of `count` increment with each click. Now open another browser to your deployed servlet using the following URL:

```
http://localhost:8080/apress/servlet/chapter3.ContextTest
```

You should see output similar to that shown in Figure 3-11.

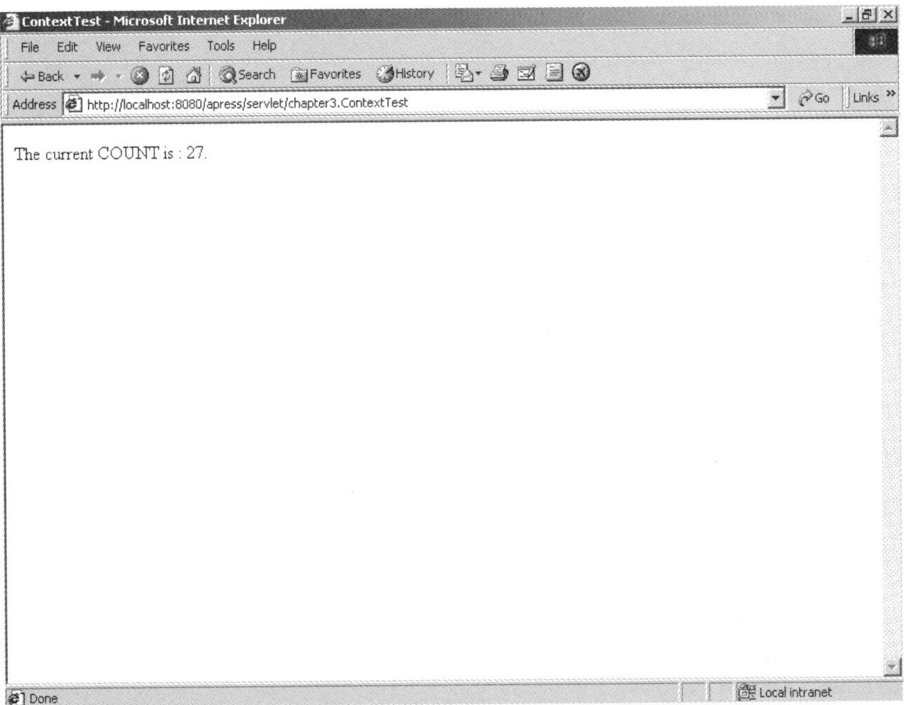

Figure 3-11. `chapter3.ContextTest` *after* `ContextTest.jsp`

The output is much the same as `ContextTest.jsp`, aside from the bold lettering, but you should notice the value of `count`. It is one greater than the last value of `count` displayed by `ContextTest.jsp`. This is because they share the same `ServletContext`. This is the "shared memory" functionality that we spoke of earlier in the chapter. You can go back and forth between the JSP and servlet, clicking on the Refresh button, and you'll see how they share the `count` object.

Now open the JSP from the `/apress2` Web application using the following URL:

```
http://localhost:8080/apress2/ContextTest.jsp
```

You'll see that the value of `count` has been reset to `0`. This is because it is a different `count`, and this is the relationship between `ServletContexts` and Web applications: the `ServletContext` associated with `/apress2` is unique to this Web application and cannot be affected by Web components in any other Web application, including `/apress`.

To conclude our example, go ahead and open the `chapter3.ContextTest` servlet that was deployed to the `/apress2` Web application using the following URL:

```
http://localhost:8080/apress2/servlet/chapter3.ContextTest
```

You'll see that it uses the same reference to the `count` attribute as the JSP deployed to `/apress2`.

NOTE *Objects stored in the* `ServletContext` *remain available for the life of the Web application.*

Summary

In this chapter, we covered the main Web application components that can be hosted in a Tomcat container. We described the Java servlet architecture and how it can be used. We then went on to describe JavaServer pages and their components. We concluded by defining the `ServletContext` and its more common uses. We described the relationship that exists between the `ServletContext` and a Web application. We also covered examples that showed how each of these topics actually perform.

In the next chapter, we begin our discussions on Tomcat's `/manager` Web application.

CHAPTER 4

Using Tomcat's Manager Application

IN THIS CHAPTER, we

- Define the Tomcat Manager Web application
- Describe the steps involved in accessing the Tomcat Manager Web application
- Discuss using the Tomcat Manager Web application

Now that you have completed a manual installation, this chapter covers the creation, deployment, and management of Web applications using Tomcat's Manager Web application. We'll walk through each of the commands available in the `/manager` Web application.

What is the Manager Web Application?

The Tomcat Manager Web application is packaged with the Tomcat server. It is installed in the context path of `/manager` and provides the basic functionality to manage Web applications running in the Tomcat server. Some of the provided functionality includes the ability to install, start, stop, remove, and report on Web applications.

NOTE *The Tomcat* `/manager` *application services only HTTP GET requests. This makes it possible to easily attach a scripting or graphical type interface as a front end to all of its functionality.*

Gaining Access to the Manager Web Application

Before you can use the Manager, you must set up a new user with the appropriate privileges to access the /manager application. If you look at the TOMCAT_HOME/webapps/manager/web.xml file in the /manager application, you'll notice a security constraint similar to the following code snippet:

```
<!-- Define a Security Constraint on this Application -->
<security-constraint>
    <web-resource-collection>
      <web-resource-name>Entire Application</web-resource-name>
      <url-pattern>/*</url-pattern>
    </web-resource-collection>
    <auth-constraint>
       <!-- NOTE:  This role is not present in the default users file -->
       <role-name>manager</role-name>
    </auth-constraint>
</security-constraint>
```

The <security-constraint/> element defined in this code snippet secures the entire /manager Web application, providing access to only those users who have a defined role of manager. It does this with essentially two sub-elements in the security constraint.

The first sub-element, <web-resource-collection>, defines the resource that is protected by this constraint. The definition is made with the <url-pattern> sub-element. When you look at the previous snippet, you'll also notice that this sub-element is defined as follows:

```
<url-pattern>/*</url-pattern>
```

The value of the <url-pattern> sub-element uses a wildcard *, which protects all URLs within the /manager application with this security constraint.

The second sub-element defines the role that has access to the protected resource. It does this by using the <role-name> sub-element, which is listed in the following code snippet:

```
<role-name>manager</role-name>
```

The value of this sub-element states that only users with a role of manager can access the resource protected by this security constraint.

What this all boils down to is that, if you want access to the manager application, you need to add a new user with a role of manager. You add such a user by inserting an entry in the TOMCAT_HOME/conf/tomcat-users.xml file, which contains all of the defined users in Tomcat. If you haven't changed this file before, it should look similar to the following code snippet:

```
<!--
  NOTE:  By default, no user is included in the "manager" role required
  to operate the "/manager" web application.  If you wish to use this app,
  you must define such a user - the username and password are arbitrary.
-->
<tomcat-users>
  <user name="tomcat" password="tomcat" roles="tomcat" />
  <user name="role1"  password="tomcat" roles="role1"  />
  <user name="both"   password="tomcat" roles="tomcat,role1" />
</tomcat-users>
```

As you can see, there is nothing special about this file: it has a root-level element of `<tomcat-users>`, which contains a collection of `<user>` sub-elements. To add a new user with access to the `manager` application, you simply need to add a new `<user>` sub-element with a `roles` attribute equal to `manager`. Listing 4-1 contains the modified `tomcat-users.xml` file, with a new user that has access to the `manager` application.

Listing 4-1. The `tomcat-users.xml` *File*

```
<!--
  NOTE:  By default, no user is included in the "manager" role required
  to operate the "/manager" web application.  If you wish to use this app,
  you must define such a user - the username and password are arbitrary.
-->
<tomcat-users>
  <user name="tomcat" password="tomcat" roles="tomcat" />
  <user name="role1"  password="tomcat" roles="role1"  />
  <user name="both"   password="tomcat" roles="tomcat,role1" />
  <user name="bob"   password="password" roles="manager" />
</tomcat-users>
```

Make the previously listed changes and save the `tomcat-users.xml` file. You now have a new user named `bob`, with a password of `password` and the role of `manager`. After making this change, restart Tomcat.

Using the Manager Web Application

After you have a privileged user, you can begin looking at the functionality that's associated with the `/manager` application, which currently has seven available commands:

- `install`
- `list`
- `reload`
- `sessions`
- `start`
- `stop`
- `remove`

We will discuss each of these commands in relation to our `apress.war` file from Chapter 2.

NOTE *Before you begin using these commands, make sure you have backed up and removed the* `/apress` *Web application from your current Tomcat installation. You should also remove the* `apress context` *entry from the* `TOMCAT_HOME/conf/server.xml` *file. This will preserve any changes that you made in Chapter 3.*

install

The first command you are going to use is `install`, which is used to deploy new Web applications. The command accepts two parameters: `war` and `path`. The first parameter, `war`, is a URL that references a WAR file or directory that contains a Web application. The second parameter, `path`, is a context path that the Web application will be attached to. We are going to use the `install` command to install and deploy our `/apress` Web application. So, you need to find the `apress.war` file from Chapter 2 and enter the following URL into your Web browser, replacing `D:\Chapter2\` with the location of your `apress.war` file.

NOTE *The* `install` *command takes the referenced WAR file and extracts it into the* `/webapps` *directory during this process. However, it does not add a new* `<Context>` *entry into the* `server.xml`.

```
http://localhost:8080/manager/install?path=/apress&war=jar:file:D:/Chapter2/
apress.war!/
```

The first time you enter a `manager` command, you are asked for a username and password. Enter the values `bob` and `password`, respectively, and click on OK. If everything was entered correctly, you should see a screen similar to that shown in Figure 4-1.

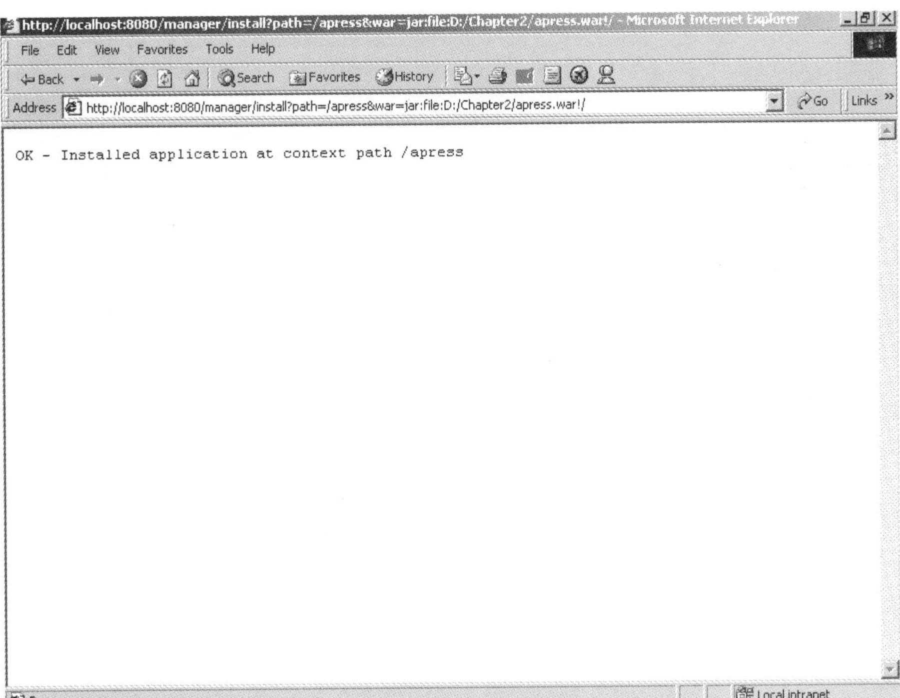

Figure 4-1. A successful `manager` *deployment*

The `install` command can be subdivided into the following pieces:

- `http://localhost:8080/manager/install`: This is the URL to the Web application `install` command.

- `path=/apress`: The `path` parameter tells the `manager` that it should install the Web application to the `/apress` context path.

- `war=jar:file:D:/Chapter2/apress.war!/`: The `war` parameter references the location of the WAR file that contains the `/apress` application. The `war` parameter is a URL that must match one of the syntax patterns described in Table 4-1, depending upon which deployment target you are using.

Table 4-1. The `war` *Parameter Syntax*

DIRECTORY	DESCRIPTION
`file:/absolutepath`	Use this syntax when deploying the Web application from a local directory. The value must be the absolute path to the root directory of the Web application.
`jar:/file:/absolutepath/warfile.war!/`	Use this syntax when deploying a WAR file from a local directory. The value must be the absolute path to the WAR file containing the Web application that is being deployed.
`jar:http://hostname:port/relativepath/warfile.war!/`	Use this syntax when deploying a WAR file that exists on a remote server. The value must be the server and port plus the relative path to the WAR file containing the Web application that is being deployed.

NOTE *You should notice that all WAR file deployments end with a* `!/`.

To test this deployment, open your browser to the following URL (which you may recognize from Chapter 2):

```
http://localhost:8080/apress/login.jsp
```

You should see the login page from Chapter 3.

list

The `list` command is used to display a list of currently deployed Web applications. The `list` command displays the name of the Web application along with two additional pieces of information: it describes the current status of the application (either `running` or `stopped`), and it displays the current number of active sessions for each application. To see the `command` in action, open your browser to the following URL:

```
http://localhost:8080/manager/list
```

You should see a page similar to that shown in Figure 4-2.

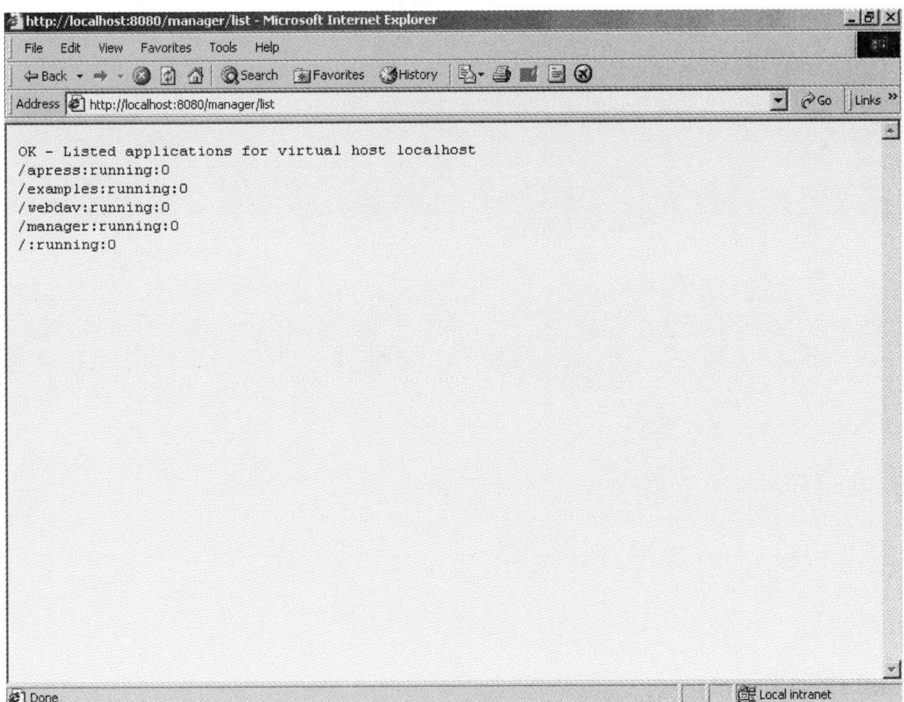

Figure 4-2. Results from the `list` *command*

`reload`

The `reload` command is used to reload all of the Web components—including servlet, JSPs, and dependent classes—associated with the named Web application. The only parameter used by the `reload` command is `path`, which names the Web application to reload. To reload all of the components associated with the `/apress` Web application, open your browser to the following URL:

```
http://localhost:8080/manager/reload?path=/apress
```

Once all of the components have been reloaded, the `manager` application responds with a page similar to that shown in Figure 4-3.

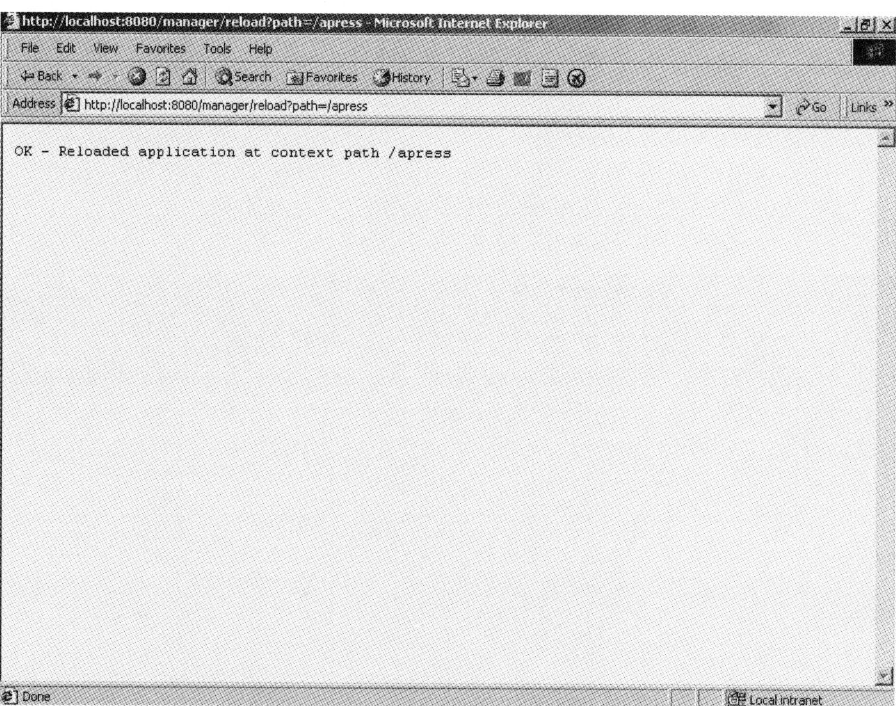

Figure 4-3. Results from the `reload` *command*

`sessions`

The `sessions` command is used to display session information associated with a named Web application. The only parameter used by the `sessions` command is `path`, which names the Web application to report upon. To display session information about the `/apress` Web application, open your browser to the following URL:

```
http://localhost:8080/manager/sessions?path=/apress
```

Once the `manager` application has gathered the session information associated with the /apress Web application, it responds with a page similar to that shown in Figure 4-4.

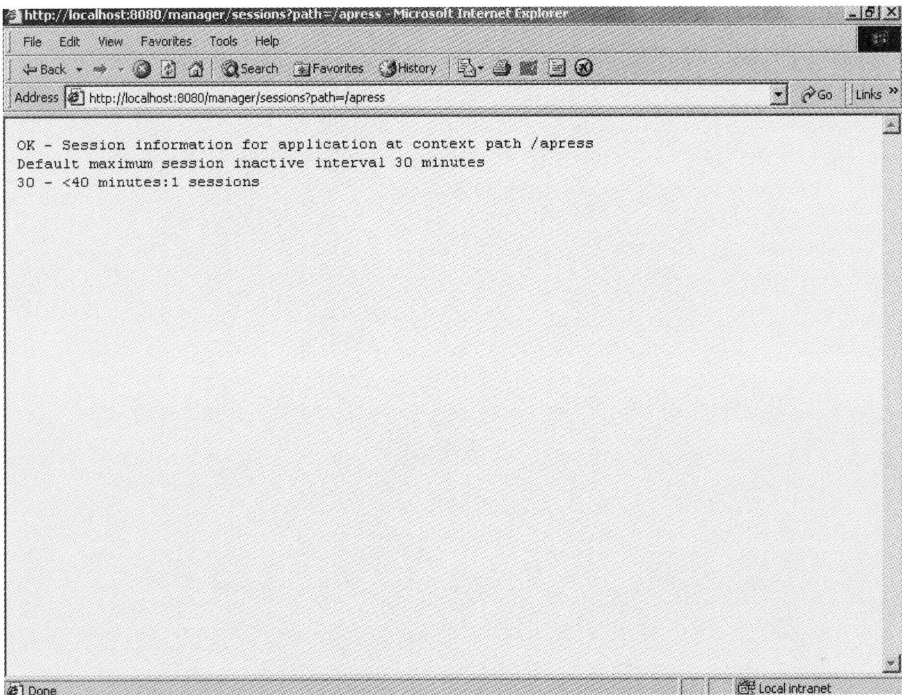

Figure 4-4. Results from the `sessions` *command*

`stop`

The `stop` command does just what you think it does: it stops the named Web application. The only parameter used by the `stop` command is `path`, which names the Web application to stop. To stop the `/apress` Web application, open your browser to the following URL:

```
http://localhost:8080/manager/stop?path=/apress
```

The `stop` command responds with a page similar to that shown in Figure 4-5.

NOTE *Once you have executed the* `stop` *command on a Web application, it won't be available until the* `start` *command has been executed with the same* `path` *value. The current status can be viewed by using the* `list` *command.*

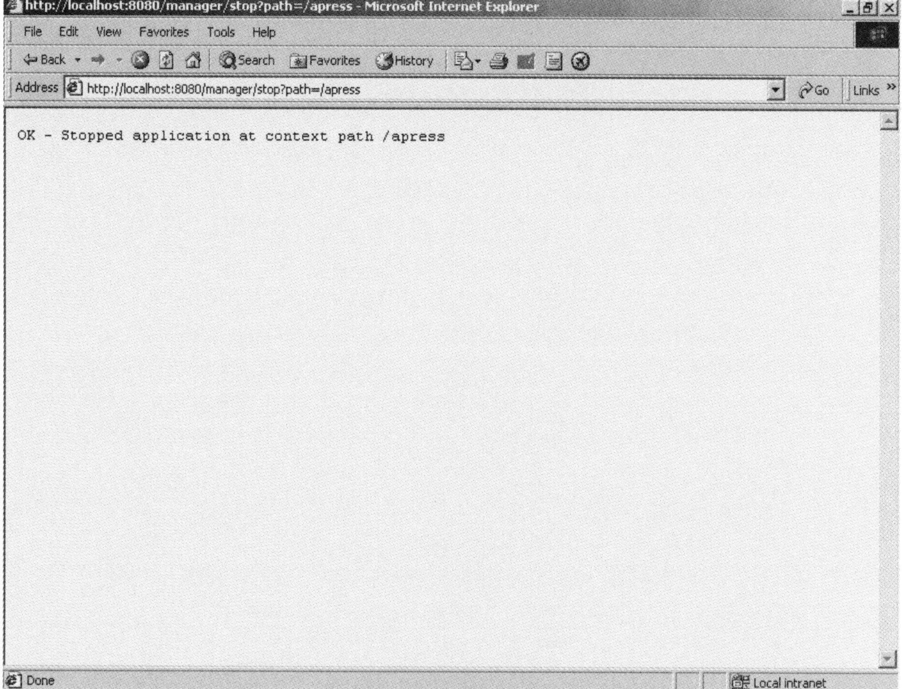

Figure 4-5. Results from the `stop` *command*

`start`

The `start` command also does just what it sounds like: it starts a named Web application that has been previously stopped. Again, the only parameter used by the `stop` command is `path`, which names the Web application to start. To start the previously stopped `/apress` Web application, open your browser to the following URL:

```
http://localhost:8080/manager/start?path=/apress
```

Once all of the components have been reloaded, the `manager` application responds with a page similar to that shown in Figure 4-6.

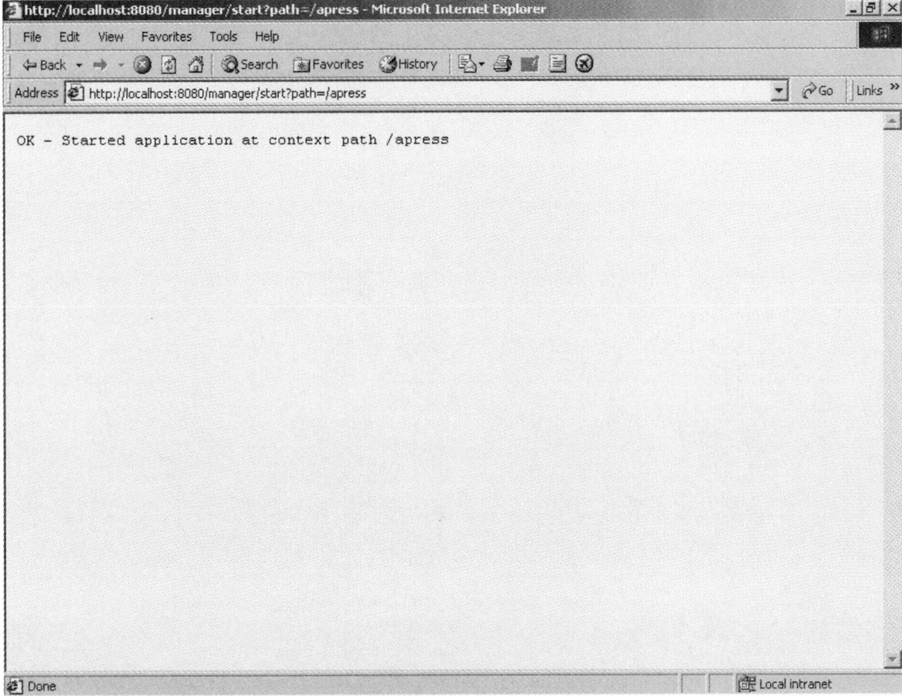

Figure 4-6. Results from the `start` *command*

`remove`

The last command that you will use, appropriately enough, is the `remove` command. It is used to stop and remove the named Web application from the Tomcat server. It does not remove the directories and files associated with the Web application, however; it simply removes the application from the internally maintained list of deployed applications. The `path` parameter—the only one used by this command as well—names the Web application to remove. To remove all of the components associated with the `/apress` Web application, open your browser to the following URL:

```
http://localhost:8080/manager/remove?path=/apress
```

Once all of the components have been removed, the `manager` application responds with a page similar to that shown in Figure 4-7.

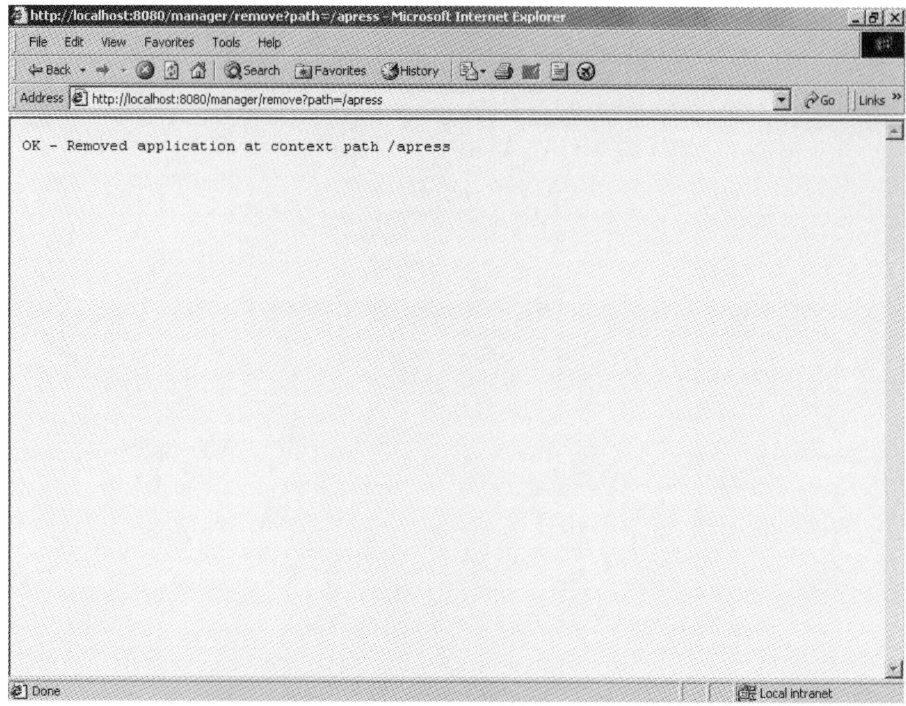

Figure 4-7. Results from the `remove` *command*

NOTE *If you are testing all of these commands on the* `/apress` *Web application, you may want to test the* `remove` *command last. This is to prevent you from removing the Web application while there are still other commands to be executed.*

Summary

In this chapter, we covered using the Tomcat `/manager` Web application to install and manage our own Web application. We defined the `/manager` Web application and discussed each of the available commands. In the next chapter, we cover securing Tomcat with realms.

CHAPTER 5

Configuring Security Realms

IN THIS CHAPTER, we

- Define security realms
- Describe memory realms
- Describe JDBC realms
- Discuss how you can access user data after authentication

In this chapter we cover some of the methods that Tomcat provides for protecting resources. First, we talk about using security realms to protect a resource. Then, we move on to the types of security realms that Tomcat uses, namely Memory and JDBC realms.

Security Realms

A *security realm* is a mechanism for protecting Web application resources. It gives you the ability to protect a resource with a defined security constraint and then define the user roles that can access the protected resource.

Tomcat contains this type of realm functionality as a built-in feature, and the `org.apache.catalina.Realm` interface is the component that provides this functionality. The interface provides a mechanism by which a collection of usernames, passwords, and their associated roles can be integrated into Tomcat. If you downloaded the Tomcat source, you can find this interface in the following location:

```
<TOMCAT_HOME>/src/catalina/src/share/org/apache/catalina/Realm.java
```

Tomcat 4 provides two classes of `Realm` implementations: `MemoryRealm` and `JDBCRealm`. We discuss each implementation in the following sections.

Memory Realms

The first Realm implementation provided with Tomcat is a memory realm, which is implemented by the org.apache.catalina.realm.MemoryRealm class. The MemoryRealm class uses a simple XML file as a container of users. The following code snippet contains an example memory realm XML file:

```
<!--
  NOTE:  By default, no user is included in the "manager" role required
  to operate the "/manager" web application.  If you wish to use this app,
  you must define such a user - the username and password are arbitrary.
-->
<tomcat-users>
  <user name="tomcat" password="tomcat" roles="tomcat" />
  <user name="role1"  password="tomcat" roles="role1"  />
  <user name="both"   password="tomcat" roles="tomcat,role1" />
  <user name="bob"   password="password" roles="manager" />
</tomcat-users>
```

NOTE *The default location of the* MemoryRealms *XML file is the* <TOMCAT_HOME>/conf/tomcat-users.xml. *You can change the location of this file by substituting a new relative or absolute path in the* pathname *attribute of the* <Realm> *element described in the following section.*

As you can see, this file contains nothing terribly complicated. It has a root element of <tomcat-users>, which contains *n*-number of the sub-element <user>. The <user> element contains all of the necessary information to validate a user. This information is contained in the attributes of the <user> sub-element. Table 5-1 contains a description of each of the attributes required in the <user> sub-element.

Table 5-1. The Required Attributes of the `<user>` *Sub-Element*

ATTRIBUTE	DESCRIPTION
name	Contains a string representing the username that will be used in the login form
password	Contains a string representing the password that will be used in the login form
roles	Contains the role(s) assigned to the named user. This is the value that must match the `<role-name>` sub-element of the security constraint defined in the Web application's `web.xml` file. If more than one role is assigned to the user, the value of the `roles` attribute must contain a comma-separated list of roles.

Protecting a Resource with a MemoryRealm

To actually see how a `MemoryRealm` works, let's create a realm that protects our `/apress` application. The steps involved in setting up a new `MemoryRealm` are as follows:

1. Open the `<TOMCAT_HOME>/conf/server.xml` and make sure that the following line is not commented out.

```
<Realm className="org.apache.catalina.realm.MemoryRealm" />
```

By ensuring that this `<Realm>` entry is not commented out, you are making the `MemoryRealm` the default realm implementation for the entire default container.

NOTE *If you cannot find this entry, add it directly under the* `Engine` *sub-element.*

2. Open the `<TOMCAT_HOME>/webapps/apress/WEB-INF/web.xml` file and add the following security constraint as the last sub-element of `<web-app>`:

```
   <!-- Define a Security Constraint on this Application -->
<security-constraint>
  <web-resource-collection>
```

```
    <web-resource-name>Apress Application</web-resource-name>
    <url-pattern>/*</url-pattern>
  </web-resource-collection>
  <auth-constraint>
     <role-name>apressuser</role-name>
  </auth-constraint>
</security-constraint>
```

NOTE *Tomcat throws an* `org.xml.sax.SAXParseException` *if this entry is not added to the end of the* `web.xml` *file.*

You need to focus on only two sub-elements: `<url-pattern>` and `<role-name>`. The `<url-pattern>` sub-element defines the URL pattern that is to be protected by the resource. The entry that you include protects the entire `/apress` Web application. The second sub-element, `<role-name>`, defines the user role that can access the resource protected by the previously defined `<url-pattern>`. In summary, this entire entry states that the `/apress` Web application can be accessed only by users with a defined role of `apressuser`.

3. Add the following `<login-config>` sub-element directly after the `<security-constraint>`.

```
<!-- Define the Login Configuration for this Application -->
<login-config>
     <auth-method>BASIC</auth-method>
          <realm-name>Apress Application</realm-name>
</login-config>
```

The `<login-config>` sub-element simply defines the authentication method for the defined realm. The possible values are `BASIC`, `DIGEST`, and `FORM`.

4. Open the `<TOMCAT_ROOT>/conf/tomcat-users.xml` file and add the following `<user>` sub-element:

```
<user name="robert" password="password" roles="apressuser" />
```

The <user> sub-element you are adding creates a new user in the MemoryRealm database with a name of robert, a password of password, and a role of apressuser. You should notice that the value of the roles attribute matches the value of the <role-name> sub-element of the previously defined <sercurity-contstraint>.

5. To complete this configuration, stop and restart the Tomcat server.

Now let's actually look at how your newly defined realm affects the /apress Web application. Point your browser to the following URL:

```
http://localhost:8080/apress/login.jsp
```

If everything went according to plan, you should see a dialog box similar to Figure 5-1.

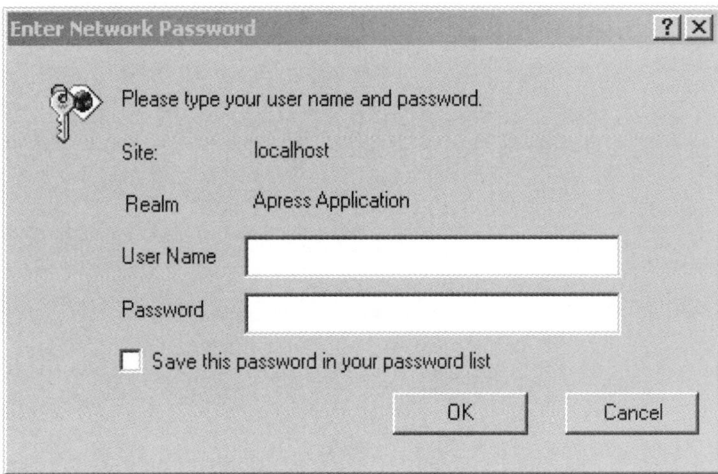

Figure 5-1. The BASIC *authentication dialog will prompt you for a user ID and password.*

Go ahead and enter robert for the username and password for the password, and click on OK. Again, if everything goes according to plan, you should see the login page of the /apress Web application. You now have a Web application that is protected by a security realm that uses the basic authentication method to authenticate its users.

JDBC Realms

The second Realm implementation provided with Tomcat is a JDBC realm, which is implemented by the org.apache.catalina.realm.JDBCRealm class. This class is much like the MemoryRealm discussed in the previous section, with the exception of where it stores its collection of users. A JDBCRealm stores all of its users in a user-defined and JDBC-compliant database. Setting up a JDBC realm involves several steps, but it is really simple to manage once it is configured.

Creating the Users Database

Before you begin configuring Tomcat to use a JDBCRealm, you must first create a database to hold your collection of users. For this example, we are configuring both a MySQL database and a Microsoft Access database.

NOTE *If you already have a database of users, you can substitute the values we are using here with the appropriate values relating to your database. If you do not have an existing database, you can find the Access database or SQL Scripts to create the MySQL database with the rest of the source code at* http://www.virtuas.com/publications.html.

Our user database is going to contain three tables. The first table is the users table, which contains the username and password for each of our users. Table 5-2 contains the description of the users table.

Table 5-2. The users *Table Definition*

COLUMN	DESCRIPTION
user_name	Contains a string representing the username that will be used in the login form. It has a type of varchar(12).
user_pass	Contains a string representing the user's password. It also has a type of varchar(12).

The second table in the users database is the roles table, which contains all of the possible roles for the users defined in this database. The roles table contains a single column, role_name, that is a varchar(12) representing each role name.

The last table in the users database is the user_roles table. The user_roles table is a mapping table between the roles and users defined in this database. Table 5-3 contains the table definition for the user_roles table.

Table 5-3. The user_roles *Table Definition*

COLUMN	DESCRIPTION
user_name	Contains a string referring to a user in the users table. It has a type of varchar(12).
role_name	Contains a string referring to a role in the roles table. It also has a type of varchar(12).

This is our complete database. The relationships between each of these tables are represented in Figure 5-2.

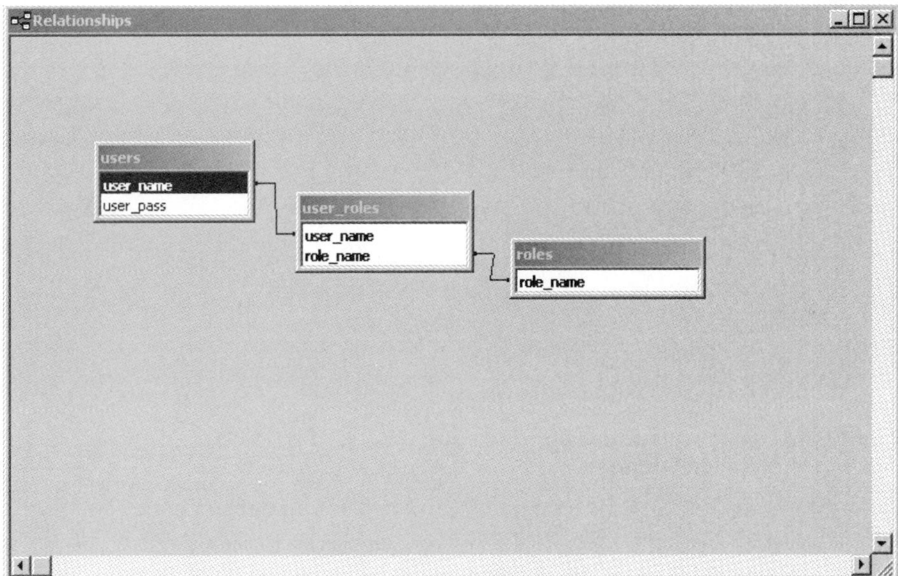

Figure 5-2. This figure shows the relationships of the tables in the user *database.*

The contents of each of the users database's tables are listed in Table 5-4, 5-5, and 5-6.

Table 5-4. The Contents of the `users` *Table*

USER_NAME	USER_PASS
bob	password
joe	joe
robert	password
tomcat	password

Table 5-5. The Contents of the `roles` *Table*

ROLE_NAME
apressuser
manager
tomcat

Table 5-6. The Contents of the `user_roles` *Table*

USER_NAME	ROLE_NAME
bob	manager
joe	apressuser
joe	manager
robert	apressuser
tomcat	tomcat

Creating and Configuring a MySQL Users Database

Before you can create the Users database in MySQL, you need to have downloaded and installed the MySQL server, which can be found at `http://www.mysql.com`. You should also download the latest JDBC driver for MySQL, which can also be found at the same Web site.

After you have MySQL installed, you need to complete the following steps to create and configure a MySQL Users database:

1. Start the `mysql` client found in the `<MYSQL_HOME>/bin/` directory.

2. Create the Users database, which will be explicitly named `tomcatusers`, by executing the following command:

```
create database tomcatusers;
```

3. Make sure that you are modifying the correct database using the following command:

```
use tomcatusers;
```

4. Create the `users` table using the following command:

```
create table users
(
        user_name varchar(15) not null primary key,
        user_pass varchar(15) not null
);
```

5. Create the `roles` table using the following command:

```
create table roles
(
        role_name varchar(15) not null primary key
);
```

6. Create the `user_roles` table using the following command:

```
create table users_roles
(
        user_name varchar(15) not null,
        role_name varchar(15) not null,
        primary key(user_name, role_name)
);
```

7. Insert the `user` data into the `users` table by executing the following commands:

```
insert into users values("bob", "password");
insert into users values("joe", "$joe$");
insert into users values("robert", "password");
insert into users values("tomcat", "password");
```

8. Insert the `roles` data into the `roles` table with the following commands:

```
insert into roles values("apressuser");
insert into roles values("manager");
insert into roles values("tomcat");
```

9. Insert the `user_roles` data into the `user_roles` table with the following commands:

```
insert into user_roles values("bob", "manager");
insert into user_roles values("joe", "apressuser");
insert into user_roles values("joe", "manager");
insert into user_roles values("robert", "apressuser");
insert into user_roles values("tomcat", "tomcat");
```

You now have a MySQL database of users. If you are not interested in the Microsoft configuration, skip the following section and continue with the "Configuring Tomcat to Use a JDBC Realm" section.

Creating and Configuring a Microsoft Access Users Database

Microsoft Access uses a single file to represent a database; therefore, you can simply use the `users.mdb` file included with this text's source code, instead of going through the steps that are normally required to create a `users` database.

Although you do not have to create the `users` database, you need to set up an ODBC data source that can be referenced by the JDBC-ODBC bridge. The following steps describe the process of setting up a new data source:

NOTE *The JDBC-ODBC bridge is a JDBC driver that is packaged with the standard JDK. It provides JDBC access to most Microsoft ODBC data sources.*

1. Open the Windows NT/2000 control panel. You should see an image similar to that shown in Figure 5-3.

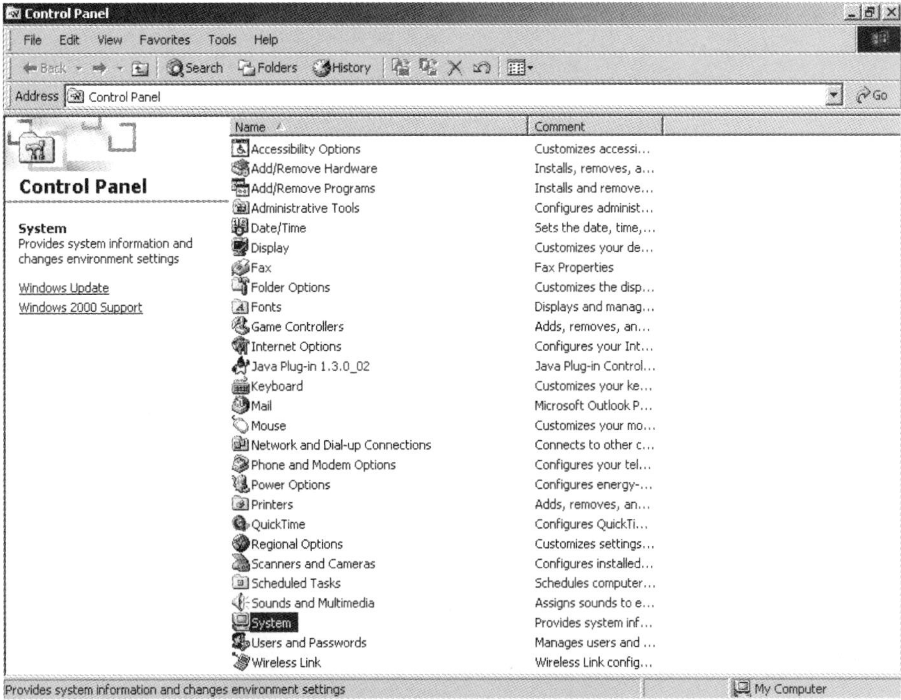

Figure 5-3. The Windows NT/2000 control panel is used to access the Administative Tools folder.

2. Double-click on the Administrative Tools icon. You should see an image similar to Figure 5-4.

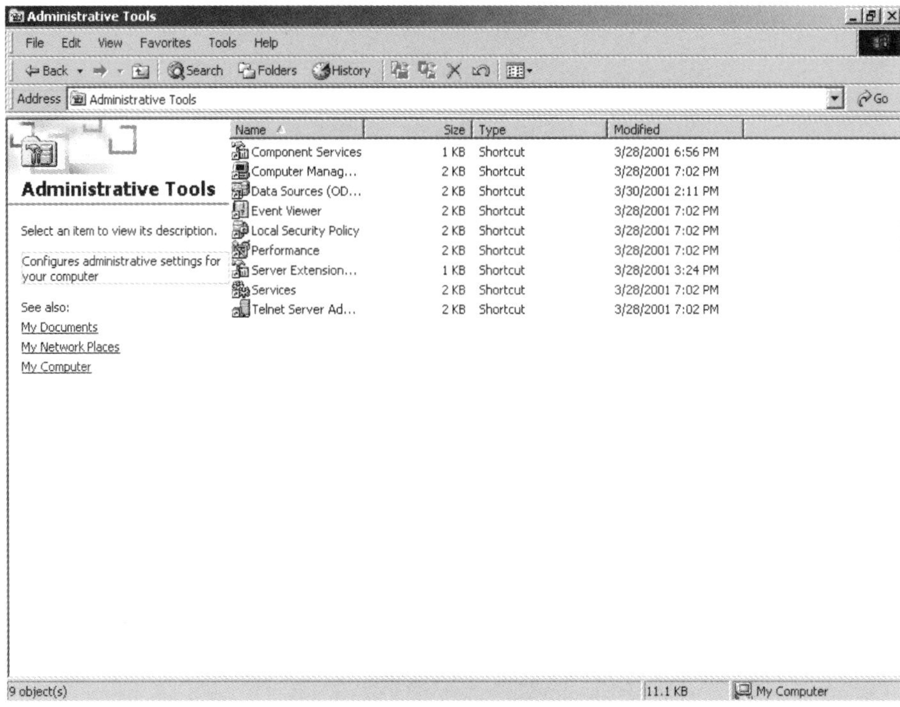

Figure 5-4. The Windows NT/2000 Administrative Tools folder contains the link to the ODBC data sources.

3. Double-click on the Data Sources (ODBC) icon and select the System DSN tab. You should see an image similar to Figure 5-5.

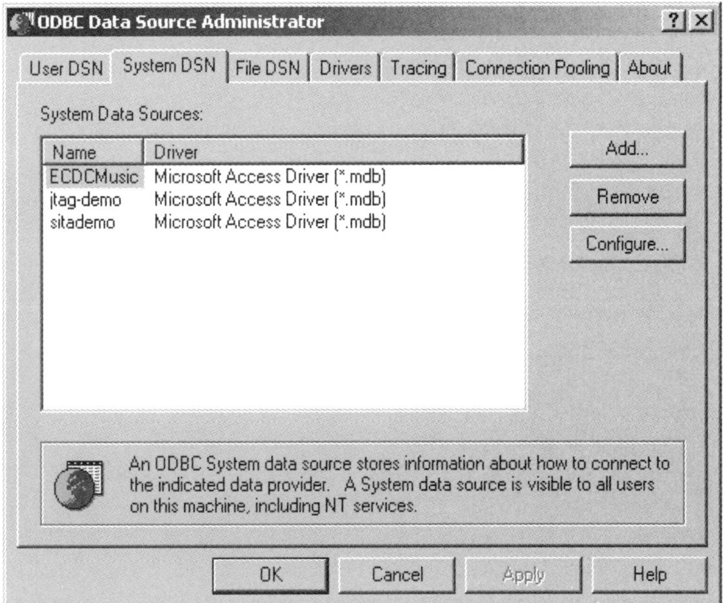

Figure 5-5. The Windows NT/2000 ODBC Data Source Administrator provides access to all of your ODBC data sources.

4. Select the Add button. You should see an image similar to Figure 5-6.

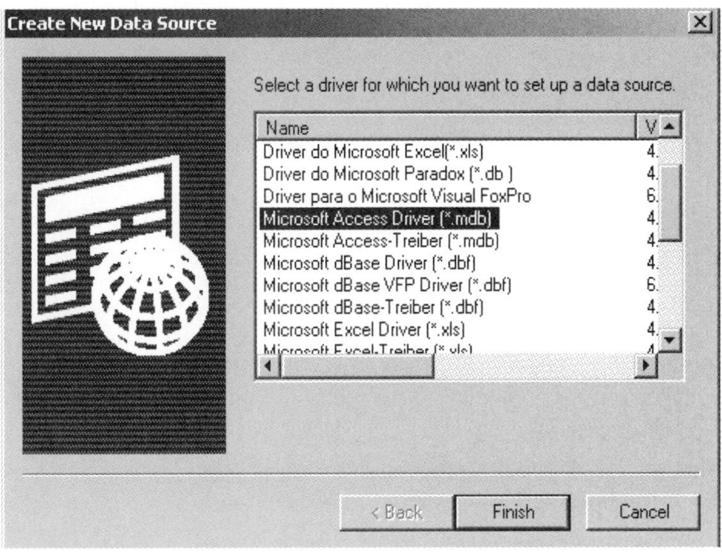

Figure 5-6. The Windows NT/2000 Create New Data Source wizard walks you through the steps of creating a new ODBC data source.

5. Select Microsoft Access and click on the Finish button. You should see an image similar to Figure 5-7.

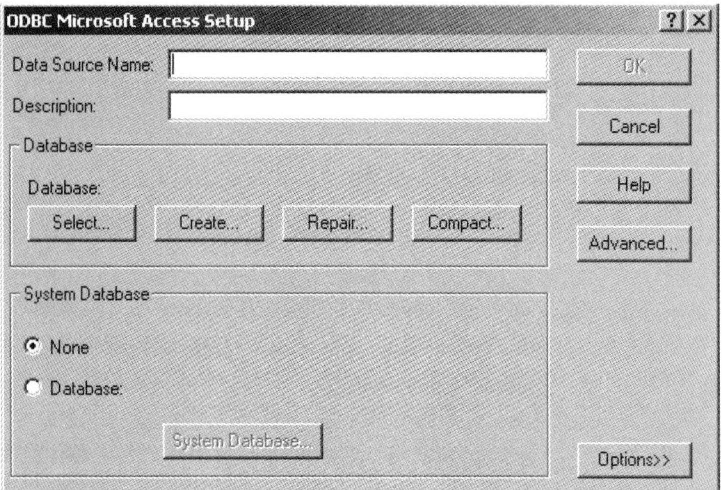

Figure 5-7. The Windows NT/2000 ODBC Microsoft Access setup dialog box shows your newly created ODBC data source.

6. Enter `jdbcRealm` in the Data Source Name edit box.

7. Click on the Select button and navigate to the location of the `users.mdb` file. Click on OK for all remaining actions.

You now have an ODBC data source that contains your database of users.

Configuring Tomcat to Use a JDBC Realm

Now that we have a container of users, let's configure Tomcat to use the JDBC container instead of the previously configured `MemoryRealm`. The steps involved in configuring a `JDBCRealm` are described in the following list:

1. Open the `<TOMCAT_HOME>/conf/server.xml` and place a comment around the previously uncommented `<Realm>` element.

```
<!-- <Realm className="org.apache.catalina.realm.MemoryRealm" /> -->
```

2. Place one of the following code snippets, based upon the database you are using, directly below the previously referenced `<Realm>` element:

Microsoft Configuration

```
<Realm className="org.apache.catalina.realm.JDBCRealm"
driverName="sun.jdbc.odbc.JdbcOdbcDriver"
connectionURL="jdbc:odbc:jdbcRealm"
userTable="users" userNameCol="user_name" userCredCol="user_pass"
userRoleTable="user_roles" roleNameCol="role_name" />
```

MySQL Configuration

```
<Realm  className="org.apache.catalina.realm.JDBCRealm" debug="99"
driverName="org.gjt.mm.mysql.Driver"
connectionURL="jdbc:mysql://localhost/tomcatusers?user=test;password=test"
userTable="users" userNameCol="user_name" userCredCol="user_pass"
      userRoleTable="user_roles" roleNameCol="role_name" />
```

NOTE *Make sure that the JAR file containing the JDBC driver referenced by the* `driverName` *attribute is placed in Tomcat's CLASSPATH. If you are using the JDBC-ODBC bridge, the driver is already in Tomcat's CLASSPATH.*

This new `<Realm>` entry defines a `JDBCRealm` that leverages one of our databases as its container of users. The attributes used in the `<Realm>` element, with additional optional attributes, are described in Table 5-7.

Table 5-7. The `<Realm>` Element Attributes

ATTRIBUTE	DESCRIPTION
`classname`	The fully qualified class name of the `Realm` implementation
`driverName`	The name of the driver used to connect to the database containing the users
`connectionURL`	The URL referencing the database containing the users
`connectionName`	(Optional) The username to use when connecting to the database. Microsoft Access does not require a username. If you are using MySQL, you can encode the username directly on the `connectionURL`.
`connectionPassword`	(Optional) The password to use when connecting to the database. Access does not require a password. If you are using MySQL, you can encode the password directly on the `connectionURL`.
`userTable`	The database table containing the user's information
`userNameCol`	The column in the `userTable` that references the user's username
`userCredCol`	The column in the `userTable` that references the user's password
`userRoleTable`	The database table containing the mapping between the `userTable` and the table containing the possible user roles
`roleNameCol`	The column in the `userRoleTable` that contains a role given to a user

3. To complete this configuration change, stop and restart the Tomcat server.

Your Web applications are now protected by a `JDBCRealm`. At this point, you should be able to log in to the `/apress` Web application by selecting from the `users` table a user who has a `role` of `apressuser`.

The Benefits of Using a JDBCRealm

JDBC realms are one of Tomcat's more exciting bits of functionality. They solve many of the authentication problems that have existed for many years. Two of the more common benefits of using a JDBC realm are as follows:

- Using a JDBC Realm makes it possible for you to leverage your application's database as a container of users, whereas, in most previously existing Web applications, the container of users exists in some proprietary Web server database.

- You can make changes to the live user database and have the changes take effect without restarting the Tomcat server. When using a `MemoryRealm`, you must restart the Tomcat server after adding new users.

Accessing an Authenticated User

Once a user has been authenticated, it is very easy to access the user's information using the `HttpServletRequest` interface. Because the user's information is stored in the `HttpServletRequest` object, it is available to all JSPs and servlets existing in the same request. To see how this information is accessed, we are going to change the `welcome.jsp` page from Chapter 2. The modified `welcome.jsp` can be found in Listing 5-1.

Listing 5-1. The Modified `welcome.jsp` *Page*

```
<html>
<head>
  <title>Apress Demo</title>
  <meta http-equiv="Content-Type" content="text/html; charset=iso-8859-1">
</head>

  <table width="500" border="0" cellspacing="0" cellpadding="0">
    <tr>
      <td> </td>
    </tr>
    <tr>
    <td>
      <img src="/apress/images/monitor2.gif"></td>
    <td>
      <b><apress:hello /> : <%= request.getRemoteUser() %></b>
    </td>
    </tr>
    <tr>
      <td> </td>
```

```
    </tr>
  </table>
</body>
</html>
```

The only code you need to examine, from the modified JSP, is the following code snippet:

```
<b><apress:hello /> : <%= request.getRemoteUser() %></b>
```

NOTE *The* `request` *object is a reference to the current* `HttpServletRequest` *object. It is implicitly available to all JSPs.*

This code uses the `request.getRemoteUser()` method to retrieve the authenticated user's `username`. It then outputs the returned `username`. After you have made the changes to this JSP, copy it to the `<TOMCAT_HOME>/webapps/apress/` directory and point your browser to the following URL:

```
http://localhost:8080/apress/welcome.jsp.
```

If you have already been authenticated, you should see the screen shown in Figure 5-8 with the `username` with which you were authenticated following the `Hello` text. If you have not been authenticated in the `/apress` Web application, enter `robert` and `password` in the BASIC authentication dialog box. You should then see the screen shown in Figure 5-8 with `robert` following the `Hello` text.

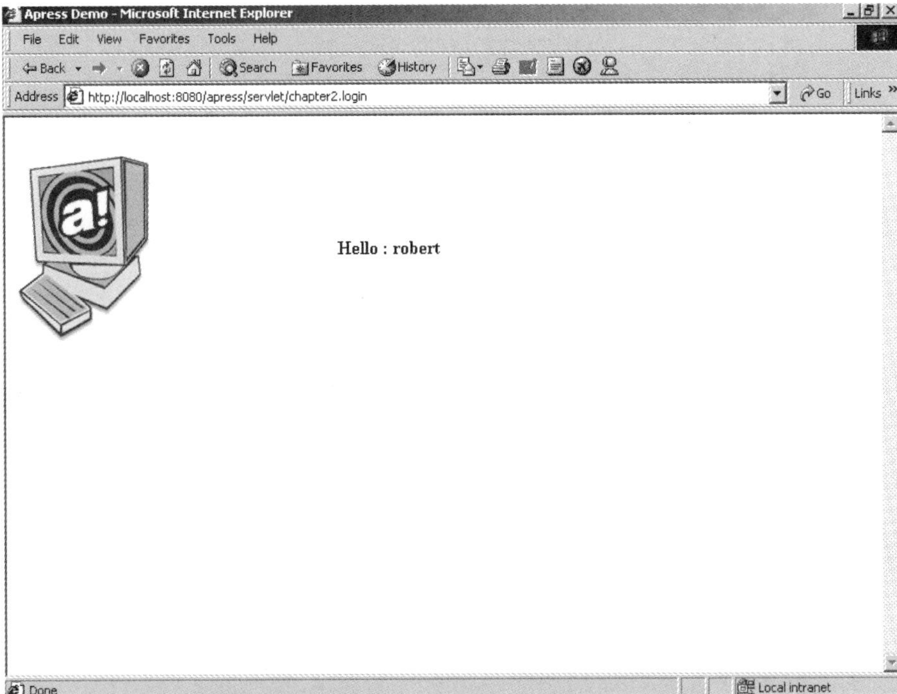

Figure 5-8. The Modified `welcome.jsp` *page shows the effect of retrieving the username from a security realm.*

Summary

We discussed security realms and how they are used, and we also covered the two types of security realms that are packaged with Tomcat (memory realms and JDBC realms), including their configuration and use. In the next chapter, we cover securing a Web application using the Secure Sockets Layer (SSL).

CHAPTER 6

Embedding Tomcat

IN THIS CHAPTER, we

- Discuss the steps to build an embedded Tomcat application
- Create a sample application that contains an embedded version of Tomcat

Embedding Tomcat into a Java Application

To create a Java application that contains an embedded version of the Tomcat server, we will leverage some existing Tomcat classes that have been developed to ease this type of integration.

The main class we want to use is `org.apache.catalina.startup.Embedded`, which can be found in the `<CATALINA_HOME>/src/catalina/src/share/org/apache/catalina/startup` directory. You can open this file and skim over it. (You don't need to examine it in too much detail.) We will look at certain parts of the `Embedded` object as we leverage it to build our own application.

Recall from Chapter 1 that Tomcat can be subdivided into a set of containers with each having their own purpose. These containers are by default configured using the `server.xml` file. When embedding a version of Tomcat, you won't have this file available, and so you need to assemble instances of these containers programmatically. The following XML code snippet, from the `server.xml` file, contains the hierarchy of the Tomcat containers:

```
<Server port="8005" shutdown="SHUTDOWN" debug="0">

  <Service name="Tomcat-Standalone">

    <Connector className="org.apache.catalina.connector.http.HttpConnector"
      port="8080" minProcessors="5" maxProcessors="75"
      enableLookups="true" redirectPort="8443"
      acceptCount="10" debug="0" connectionTimeout="60000"/>

    <Engine name="Standalone" defaultHost="localhost" debug="0">
```

```
      <Host name="localhost" debug="0" appBase="webapps" unpackWARs="true">

        <Context path="/examples" docBase="examples" debug="0"
          reloadable="true">
        </Context>

      </Host>

    </Engine>

  </Service>

</Server>
```

This is the structure that we need to create with our embedded application. Because the <Server> and <Service> elements of this structure are implicitly created, we don't need to create these objects ourselves. The steps to create this container structure are as follows:

1. Create an instance of `org.apache.catalina.Engine`. This object represents the previous <Engine> element and acts as a container to the <Host> element.

2. Create an `org.apache.catalina.Host` object, which represents a virtual host, and add this instance to the `Engine` object.

3. Now you need to create *N*-number of `org.apache.catalina.Context` objects that will represent each Web application in this `Host`. Add each of the created `Contexts` to the previously created `Host`.

4. Create an `org.apache.catalina.Connector` object and associate it with the previously created `Engine`.

These are the steps that we must perform to create our own application containing an embedded version of the Tomcat server. Listing 6-1 reveals our sample application that builds these containers using the provided `Embedded` class.

Listing 6-1. `EmbeddedTomcat.java`

```
package chapter6;

import java.net.URL;
```

```
import org.apache.catalina.Connector;
import org.apache.catalina.Context;
import org.apache.catalina.Deployer;
import org.apache.catalina.Engine;
import org.apache.catalina.Host;
import org.apache.catalina.logger.SystemOutLogger;
import org.apache.catalina.startup.Embedded;
import org.apache.catalina.Container;

public class EmbeddedTomcat {

  private String path = null;

  private Embedded embedded = null;
  private Host host = null;

  /**
    * Default Constructor
    *
    */
  public EmbeddedTomcat() {

  }

  /**
    * Basic Accessor setting the value of the context path
    *
    * @param        path - the path
    */
  public void setPath(String path) {

    this.path = path;
  }

  /**
    * Basic Accessor returning the value of the context path
    *
    * @return - the context path
    */
  public String getPath() {

    return path;
  }
```

```
/**
  * This method Starts the Tomcat server.
  */
public void startTomcat() throws Exception {

  Engine engine = null;

  // Set the home directory
  System.setProperty("catalina.home", getPath());

  // Create an embedded server
  embedded = new Embedded();
  embedded.setDebug(5);
  embedded.setLogger(new SystemOutLogger());

  // Create an engine
  engine = embedded.createEngine();
  engine.setDefaultHost("localhost");

  // Create a default virtual host
  host = embedded.createHost("localhost", getPath() + "/webapps");
  engine.addChild(host);

  // Create the ROOT context
  Context context = embedded.createContext("", getPath() + "/webapps/ROOT");
  host.addChild(context);

  // Create the examples context
  Context examplesContext = embedded.createContext("/examples", getPath() +
    "/webapps/examples");

  host.addChild(examplesContext);

  // Install the assembled container hierarchy
  embedded.addEngine(engine);

  // Assemble and install a default HTTP connector
  Connector connector = embedded.createConnector(null, 8080, false);
  embedded.addConnector(connector);

  // Start the embedded server
  embedded.start();
}
```

```
/**
  * This method Stops the Tomcat server.
  */
public void stopTomcat() throws Exception {

  // Stop the embedded server
  embedded.stop();
}

/**
  * Registers a WAR
  *
  * @param contextPath - the context path under which the
  *                application will be registered
  * @param url - the URL of the WAR file to be registered.
  */
public void registerWAR(String contextPath, URL url) throws Exception {

  if ( contextPath == null ) {

    throw new Exception("Invalid Path : " + contextPath);
  }
  String displayPath = contextPath;
  if( contextPath.equals("/") ) {

    contextPath = "";
  }

  if ( url == null ) {

    throw new Exception("Invalid WAR : " + url);
  }

  Deployer deployer = (Deployer)host;
  Context context = deployer.findDeployedApp(contextPath);

  if (context != null) {

    throw new Exception("Context " + contextPath + " already Exists!");
  }
  deployer.install(contextPath, url);
}
```

```
  /**
   * removes a WAR
   *
   * @param contextPath - the context path to be removed
   */
  public void unregisterWAR(String contextPath) throws Exception {

    Context context = host.map(contextPath);
    if ( context != null ) {

      embedded.removeContext(context);
    }
    else {

      throw new Exception("Context does not exist for named path : "
        + contextPath);
    }
  }

  public static void main(String args[]) {

    try {

      EmbeddedTomcat tomcat = new EmbeddedTomcat();
      tomcat.setPath("d:/EmbeddedTomcat");

      tomcat.startTomcat();

      Thread.sleep(100000);

      tomcat.stopTomcat();

      System.exit(0);
    }
    catch( Exception e ) {

      e.printStackTrace();
    }
  }
}
```

You should begin your examination of the EmbeddedTomcat application source with the main() method. In this method, we first create an instance of the EmbeddedTomcat class. We then set the path of the Tomcat installation that we will be using. This path is equivalent to the <TOMCAT_HOME> environment variable. Next, this method invokes the startTomcat() method, which is the method that implements the steps we described earlier. The steps performed by this method are listed below:

NOTE *Make sure you use your* <TOMCAT_HOME> *as the value passed to the* setPath() *method.*

1. First, the system property is set to the value of the path attribute:

```
// Set the home directory
System.setProperty("catalina.home", getPath());
```

2. The method then creates an instance of the Embedded object and sets the debug level and current logger:

```
// Create an embedded server
embedded = new Embedded();
embedded.setDebug(5);
embedded.setLogger(new SystemOutLogger());
```

NOTE *When deploying a production Web application, the debug level should be* 0. *This improves performance considerably.*

3. Next, the method creates an instance of an org.apache.catalina.Engine and sets the name of the default host:

```
// Create an engine
engine = embedded.createEngine();
engine.setDefaultHost("localhost");
```

4. After an Engine has been instantiated, we create an org.apache.catalina.Host object, named localhost with a path pointing to the <TOMCAT_HOME>/webapps/ directoy, and add it the Engine object.

```
// Create a default virtual host
host = embedded.createHost("localhost", getPath() + "/webapps");
engine.addChild(host);
```

NOTE *The path value used to create this host is the root path of the created host.*

5. The next step performed by this method is to create the org.apache.catalina.Context objects, adding each of the created Contexts to the previously created Host. In this method, we are creating two Contexts: ROOT and /examples. These are the Web applications that are installed by default.

```
// Create the ROOT context
Context context = embedded.createContext("",
getPath() + "/webapps/ROOT");
host.addChild(context);

// Create the examples context
Context examplesContext = embedded.createContext("/examples",
getPath() + "/webapps/examples");
host.addChild(examplesContext);
```

6. The Engine containing the created Host and Contexts is added to the Embedded object:

```
// Install the assembled container hierarchy
embedded.addEngine(engine);
```

7. An org.apache.catalina.Connector object is created and associated with the previously created Engine:

```
// Assemble and install a default HTTP connector
Connector connector = embedded.createConnector(null, 8080, false);
embedded.addConnector(connector);
```

8. The final step is to start the Tomcat server using the `Embedded.start()` method.

When `startTomcat()` returns, the main application is put to sleep to allow the embedded server time to service requests. When the application awakens, the embedded server is stopped and the application exits.

Let's compile this application to see how it works. First, make sure all other instances of Tomcat are shut down. Now add the following JAR files, all of which can be found in the Tomcat installation, to your CLASSPATH:

- `bootstrap.jar`
- `catalina.jar`
- `crimson.jar`
- `jakarta-regexp-1.2.jar`
- `jasper-compiler.jar`
- `jasper-runtime.jar`
- `jaxp.jar`
- `jndi.jar`
- `naming.jar`
- `namingfactory.jar`
- `resources.jar`
- `servlet.jar`
- `tools.jar`

Make sure that your CLASSPATH includes the directory containing the compiled `EmbeddedTomcat`, and execute the following command:

```
java chapter6.EmbeddedTomcat
```

NOTE *I have included a stripped-down version of Tomcat as part of the source code for this text. Look in the source code for Chapter 6; the directory name is* `Embedded Tomcat`.

If everything went according to plan, you should see some log statements in the console window. When you see the following text:

```
HttpProcessor[8080][0] Starting background thread
HttpProcessor[8080][0]  Background thread has been started
HttpProcessor[8080][1] Starting background thread
HttpProcessor[8080][1]  Background thread has been started
HttpProcessor[8080][2] Starting background thread
HttpProcessor[8080][2]  Background thread has been started
HttpProcessor[8080][3] Starting background thread
HttpProcessor[8080][3]  Background thread has been started
HttpProcessor[8080][4] Starting background thread
HttpProcessor[8080][4]  Background thread has been started
```

you can access the `ROOT` and `/examples` Web applications at the following URLs, respectively:

```
http://localhost:8080/
http://localhost:8080/examples/
```

This application provides a simple example of embedding Tomcat into a Java application. If you choose to take this example further, you need to stop Tomcat upon the firing of an event instead of a simple timer.

Before we close this chapter, we need to discuss two methods in the `EmbeddedTomcat` class that we did not reference earlier: `registerWar()` and `unregisterWar()`.

The `registerWar()` method is used to deploy a new Web application. It takes two parameters: the context path of the Web application and the URL of the Web application. The values should follow the same format as the `deploy` command, described in Chapter 4 ("Using Tomcat's Manager Application"). An example that registers our `/apress` Web application is:

```
registerWar("/apress", "jar:file:D:/chapter2/apress.war!/");
```

The `unregisterWar()` method simply removes a Web application with a given `contextPath`. If we wanted to remove the previously registered `/apress` context, we would invoke this method as follows:

```
unregisterWar("/apress");
```

Summary

In this chapter, we discussed the steps of embedding Tomcat into a Java application, and then created our own example application. In the next chapter, we discuss using Tomcat's JDBC-persistent sessions.

CHAPTER 7

Persistent Sessions

IN THIS CHAPTER, we

- Define HTTP sessions and their uses
- Describe the steps involved in configuring file and JDBC persistent sessions

In this chapter, we learn about HTTP sessions and how they are used. We also look at a servlet example of using an HTTP session, and we conclude with the steps involved when configuring Tomcat to use both file and JDBC persistent HTTP sessions.

HTTP Sessions

Before we can start examining HTTP sessions, we must first understand their purpose. When the HTTP protocol—the transport mechanism of all World Wide Web transactions—was first introduced, it was intended to be only a simple request/response protocol, and no state was required to be maintained between autonomous requests. This was fine until the Web's popularity exploded.

One of the biggest demands as the Web's popularity grew was the ability to maintain—between requests—a state that is specific to each client. Several solutions to this problem are currently available: cookies, hidden form fields, and HTTP sessions. In this chapter, we focus on HTTP sessions, specifically as they relate to Java servlets.

The Servlet Implementation of HTTP Sessions

The Java Servlet SDK implements HTTP sessions using an interface named, appropriately enough, `javax.servlet.http.HttpSession`. This interface must be implemented by the servlet container. The class that implements this interface will use a unique identifier, the session ID, to look up a user's session information. This identifier is stored in the client's browser and is part of every HTTP request.

The HttpSession interface defines several methods for accessing a user's session information. Table 7-1 describes the four most popular of these methods.

Table 7-1. The Four Most Commonly Used Methods of the HttpSession *Object*

COLUMN	DESCRIPTION
getId()	The getId() method returns a java.lang.String representing the unique identifier assigned to this user's session.
invalidate()	The invalidate() method is used to invalidate this user's session, which will in turn remove all session attributes from the invalidated session.
setAttribute()	The setAttribute() method takes a name/value pair and binds the object referenced by the value parameter to this session. The name parameter is used as the key to access object. If an object is already bound to the name parameter, the object is replaced with the most recent value.
getAttribute()	The getAttribute() method takes a java.lang.String parameter, name, and returns the object bound with the specified name in this session, or null if no object is bound under the name.
getAttributeNames()	The getAttributeNames() method returns a java.util.Enumeration of java.lang.String objects containing the names of all the objects bound to this session.

NOTE *You can find more information regarding the* HttpSession *interface at* http://www.javasoft.com.

The methods described in Table 7-1 provide the basic functionality to maintain state information for a particular user. Each of these methods is used in the example found in Listing 7-1, which is a modified version of the Tomcat example servlet SessionExample. I removed some functionality to provide a more straightforward example of session management.

Listing 7-1. SessionServlet.java

```
package chapter7;

import java.io.*;
import java.text.*;
import java.util.*;
import javax.servlet.*;
import javax.servlet.http.*;

public class SessionServlet extends HttpServlet {

  public void doGet(HttpServletRequest request,
    HttpServletResponse response)
    throws IOException, ServletException {

      response.setContentType("text/html");

      PrintWriter out = response.getWriter();
      out.println("<html>");
      out.println("<body bgcolor=\"white\">");
      out.println("<head>");

      out.println("<title>Session Servlet</title>");
      out.println("</head>");
      out.println("<body>");

      // Get a reference to the HttpSession Object
      HttpSession session = request.getSession();

      // Print the current Session's ID
      out.println("Session ID:" + " " + session.getId());
      out.println("<br>");

      // Print the current Session's Creation Time
      out.println("Session Created:" + " " +
        new Date(session.getCreationTime()) + "<br>");

      // Print the current Session's Last Access Time
      out.println("Session Last Accessed" + " " +
        new Date(session.getLastAccessedTime()));

      // Get the name/value pair to be placed in the HttpSession
```

```
        String dataName = request.getParameter("name");
        String dataValue = request.getParameter("value");

        if ( dataName != null && dataValue != null ) {

          // If the Parameter Values are not null
          // then add the name/value pair to the HttpSession
          session.setAttribute(dataName, dataValue);
        }

        out.println("<P>");
        out.println("Sessions Attributes" + "<br>");

        // Get all of the Attribute Names from the HttpSession
        Enumeration names = session.getAttributeNames();

        while ( names.hasMoreElements() ) {

            String name = (String) names.nextElement();
            // Get the Attribute Value with the matching name
            String value = session.getAttribute(name).toString();
            // Print the name/value pair
            out.println(name + " = " + value + "<br>");
        }

        // Create a Form to Add name/value pairs to the HttpSession
        out.println("<P>GET based form:<br>");
        out.print("<form action=\"");
         out.print(response.encodeURL("chapter7.SessionServlet"));
        out.print("\" ");
        out.println("method=GET>");
        out.println("Session Attribute:");
        out.println("<input type=text size=20 name=name>");
        out.println("<br>");
        out.println("Session Value:");
        out.println("<input type=text size=20 name=value>");
        out.println("<br>");
        out.println("<input type=submit>");
        out.println("</form>");

        out.println("</body>");
        out.println("</html>");
    }
}
```

This SessionServlet performs some basic, but very useful, session management. Its first step is to get a reference to the HttpSession object using the following line code:

```
HttpSession session = request.getSession();
```

Once the servlet has a reference to the user's session, it prints some basic information about the session, including the unique ID representing this user's session, the creation time, and the last access time. It does this in the following code snippet:

```
// Print the current Session's ID
out.println("Session ID:" + " " + session.getId());
out.println("<br>");

// Print the current Session's Creation Time
out.println("Session Created:" + " " +
new Date(session.getCreationTime()) + "<br>");

// Print the current Session's Last Access Time
out.println("Session Last Accessed" + " " +
  new Date(session.getLastAccessedTime()));
```

The next step is where the meat of the servlet exists. It begins by retrieving the request parameters name and value. If these parameters exist, it adds them to the user's HttpSession object using the setAttribute() method as follows:

```
if ( dataName != null && dataValue != null ) {
  // If the Parameter Values are not null
  // then add the name/value pair to the HttpSession
  session.setAttribute(dataName, dataValue);
}
```

After the SessionServlet adds the new object to the session, if the parameters exist, it then gets a reference to a java.util.Enumeration that contains all of the names bound to objects in the HttpSession and prints them. This code is contained in this final snippet:

```
// Get all of the Attribute Names from the HttpSession
while ( names.hasMoreElements() ) {

  String name = (String) names.nextElement();
  // Get the Attribute Value with the matching name
```

```
        String value = session.getAttribute(name).toString();
        // Print the name/value pair
        out.println(name + " = " + value + "<br>");
      }
```

The final bit of functionality in the SessionServlet creates the form that submits new name/value pairs. You can just briefly look this code over, as it is relatively simple and does not warrant a detailed explanation.

To see this servlet in action, build the class file and move it into the <TOMCAT_HOME>/webapps/apress/WEB-INF/classes/chapter7/ directory. Next, open your browser to the following URL:

```
http://localhost:8080/apress/servlet/chapter7.SessionServlet
```

You should see a page similar to that shown in Figure 7-1. At this point, no session attributes should be listed.

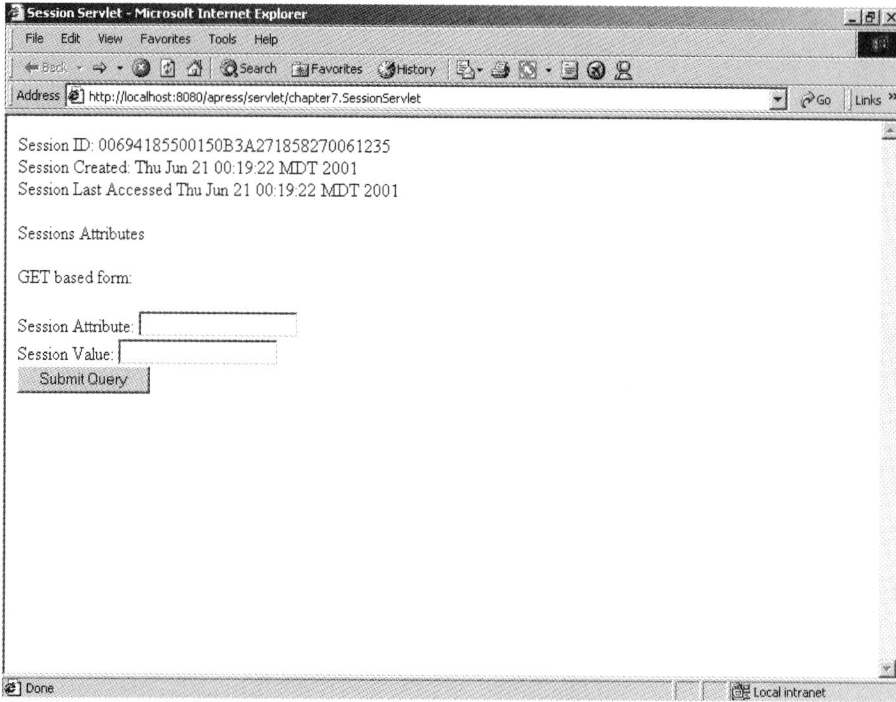

Figure 7-1. The SessionServlet*'s output with an empty HTTP session*

Now go ahead and enter some attribute/value pairs and click on the Submit button for each. You will notice with each submission that a new session attribute appears in the list. See Figure 7-2.

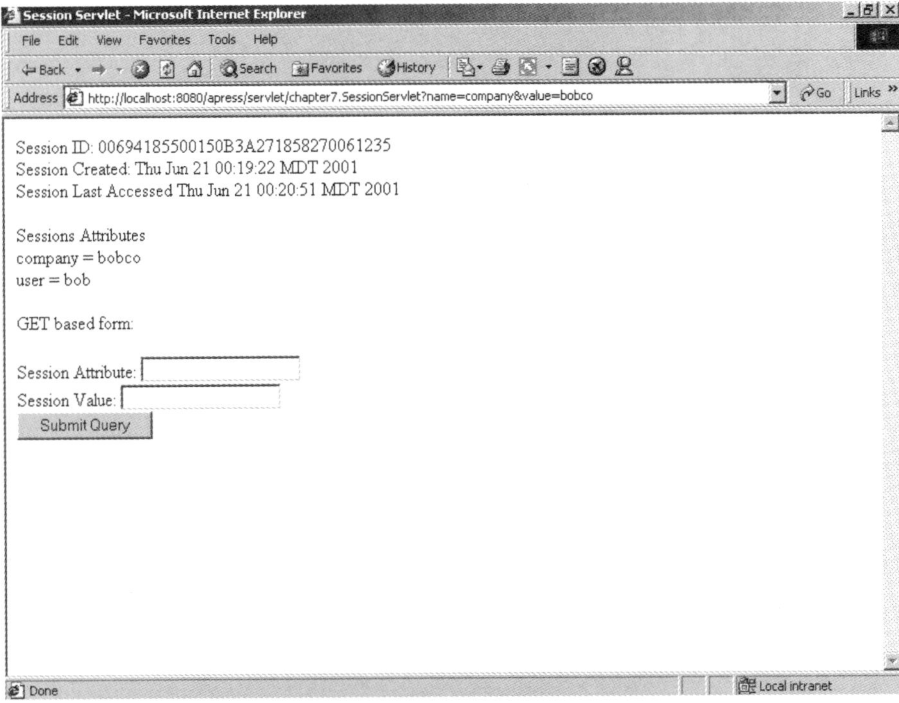

Figure 7-2. The `SessionServlet`*'s output after adding objects to the HTTP session*

This servlet provides a very simple example of HTTP state management using servlets. If you would like to learn more about servlet session management, you can find more information at `http://www.javasoft.com`.

Configuring Tomcat's Persistent Session Stores

Now that you have a grasp of what HTTP sessions are and how they are used, let's take a look at session persistence, the action of storing and retrieving HTTP session objects in a persistent data store such as a database or file system. Session persistence became an issue when session objects needed to be swapped in and out of memory based upon activity, load, and during container restarts. There needed to be a way to save and retrieve the session information when these events occurred.

Tomcat implements session persistence using the `org.apache.catalina.Store` interface. Tomcat currently comes bundled with two implementations of the `Store` interface: the `org.apache.catalina.session.FileStore` and `org.apache.catalina.session.JDBCStore`. We discuss both of these implementations in the next two sections.

The FileStore

The `FileStore` uses a file as the storage mechanism for session data. In this store, Tomcat reads and writes session information—upon startup and shutdown, respectively—from the file `<TOMCAT_HOME>/work/localhost/applicationname/Sessions.ser`.

To enable the `FileStore`, you must add a persistence manager to the Web application that is to use the session store. (A persistence manager manages Tomcat's stores.) To add a `FileStore` to our `apress` Web application, we need to add the following entry to the `apress Context` element in the `<TOMCAT_HOME%/conf/server.xml` file.

```
<Manager className="org.apache.catalina.session.PersistentManager"
  debug="0"
  saveOnRestart="true"
  maxActiveSessions="-1"
  minIdleSwap="-1"
  maxIdleSwap="-1"
  maxIdleBackup="-1">
  <Store className="org.apache.catalina.session.FileStore"/>
</Manager>
```

NOTE *If the* `/apress` *application was most recently added using the Tomcat* `/manager`*, you need to explicitly add the* `<Context>` *element to the* `server.xml` *file. You can find this entry in Chapter 2 ("Deploying Web Applications to Tomcat").*

As you examine this entry, you see several attributes associated with `Manager` (which are described in Table 7-2) and a `Store` sub-element that defines the class that actually implements the store. These `Manager` attributes define the behavior of the store that it contained.

Table 7-2. The Attributes of the `<Manager>` *Element*

ATTRIBUTE	DESCRIPTION
`className`	The `className` attribute represents the fully qualified class name of the persistent `Manager`.
`debug`	The `debug` attribute is the debug level to be used by the `Manager`.
`saveOnRestart`	The `saveOnRestart` attribute, if true, signifies that all active sessions will be saved to the persistent store when Tomcat is shut down. All sessions found in the store are reloaded upon startup. All expired sessions are ignored during shutdown and startup.
`maxActiveSessions`	The `maxActiveSessions` attribute represents the maximum number of allowed active sessions. If the number of active sessions exceeds this value, some of the sessions are swapped out to the store. We use -1, indicating that unlimited sessions are allowed.
`minIdleSwap`	The `minIdleSwap` attribute represents the minimum length of time, in seconds, that a session can remain idle before it is swapped out to the persistent store. If `minIdleSwap` equals -1, then there is no minimum time limit before a swap can occur.
`maxIdleBackup`	The `maxIdleBackup` attribute represents the length in time, in seconds, that a session can remain idle before it is backed up to the persistent store. When a session is backed up, it remains active as opposed to being swapped out, in which it is removed from the collection of active sessions. If the `maxIdleBackup` attribute is set to -1, no sessions are backed up.

To see the effects of this change, you need to restart Tomcat and then use the `SessionServlet` as described in the previous section. After you have added a few attributes to the `HttpSession`, shut Tomcat down and look in the `<TOMCAT_HOME>/work/localhost/applicationname/` directory. You should see a file named `Sessions.ser`.

The JDBCStore

The `JDBCStore` acts much the same as the `FileStore` does, with the only difference being the storage location of the session information. In this store, Tomcat reads and writes session information from the database defined in the `Store` sub-element.

Creating the Sessions Database

Before you begin configuring Tomcat to use a JDBC persistent session, you must first create a database to hold your collection of session objects. For this example, we'll create a MySQL database.

NOTE *Tomcat stores HTTP session objects as binary large objects (BLOBs), which Microsoft Access does not support. For this reason, we cannot use a Microsoft Access database in this example.*

Our database, named `tomcatsessions`, is going to contain a single table named `sessions`. Tomcat will use this table to persist HTTP session objects. Table 7-3 contains the description of the `sessions` table.

Table 7-3. The `sessions` *Table Definition*

COLUMN	DESCRIPTION
`id`	The `id` column contains a string representation of the unique session ID. The `id` has a type of `varchar(100)`.
`valid`	The `valid` column contains a single character that represents whether the session is valid or invalid. The `valid` column has a type of `char(1)`.
`maxinactive`	The `maxinactive` column contains an integer representing the length of time that a session can remain inactive before becoming invalid. The `maxinactive` column has a type of `int`.
`lastaccess`	The `lastaccess` column contains an integer that represents the length of time since the session was last accessed. The `lastaccess` column has a type of `bigint`.
`data`	The `data` column contains the serialized representation of the HTTP session. The `data` column has a type of `mediumblob`.

Before you can create the Sessions database in MySQL, you will need to have downloaded and installed the MySQL server, which can be found at `http://www.mysql.com`. You should also download the latest JDBC driver for MySQL, which can be found at the previously mentioned web site.

After you have MySQL installed, you need to complete the following steps to create and configure a MySQL Sessions database:

1. Start the `mysql` client found in the `<MYSQL_HOME>/bin/` directory.

2. Create the sessions database, which will be explicitly named `tomcatsessions`, by executing the following command:

```
create database tomcatsessions;
```

3. Make sure that you are modifying the correct database using the following command:

```
use tomcatsessions;
```

4. Create the `sessions` table using the following command:

```
create table sessions
(
  id varchar(100) not null primary key,
  valid char(1) not null,
  maxinactive int not null,
  lastaccess bigint,
  data mediumblob
);
```

NOTE *You can execute steps 2 through 4 in a single statement, using the* `createtomcatsessions.sql` *script that is packaged with this text's source code.*

You now have a MySQL database that can be used as a container for HTTP sessions objects.

Configuring Tomcat to Use a JDBCStore

To enable the `JDBCStore` for use in our `apress` Web application, you need to add the following entry to the `apress Context` element in the `<TOMCAT_HOME%/conf/server.xml` file.

NOTE *If you made the previous changes using the* `FileStore`, *you need to replace the* `Manager` *element with the one described in this section.*

```
<Manager className="org.apache.catalina.session.PersistentManager"
   debug="99"
   saveOnRestart="true"
   maxActiveSessions="-1"
   minIdleSwap="-1"
   maxIdleBackup="-1">
   <Store className="org.apache.catalina.session.JDBCStore"
     driverName="org.gjt.mm.mysql.Driver"
     connectionURL="jdbc:mysql://localhost/tomcatsessions?user=username;
password=password"
     sessionTable="sessions"
     sessionIdCol="id"
     sessionDataCol="data"
     sessionValidCol="valid"
     sessionMaxInactiveCol="maxinactive"
     sessionLastAccessedCol="lastaccess"
     checkInterval="60"
     debug="99" />
 </Manager>
```

NOTE *Make sure that the JAR file containing the JDBC driver referenced by the* `driverName` *attribute is placed in Tomcat's CLASSPATH. If you are using the JDBC-ODBC bridge, the driver will already be in Tomcat's CLASSPATH.*

This new <Store> entry defines a JDBC persistent store that leverages a database as its container of sessions. Table 7-4 describes the attributes that are used in the <Store> element and some additional optional attributes as well.

Table 7-4. The <Store> *Element Attributes*

ATTRIBUTE	DESCRIPTION
className	The className attribute represents the fully qualified class name of the Store implementation.
driverName	The driverName attribute represents the name of the driver used to connect to the database containing the sessions.
connectionURL	The connectionURL attribute represents the URL that references the database containing the sessions.
sessionTable	The sessionTable attribute represents the database table containing the HTTP session information.
sessionIdCol	The sessionIdCol attribute represents the column in the sessions table that references the unique HTTP session ID.
sessionDataCol	The sessionDataCol attribute represents the column in the sessions table that references the serialized HTTP session object.
sessionValidCol	The sessionValidCol attribute represents the column in the sessions table that signifies whether the session is valid or not.
sessionMaxInactiveCol	The sessionMaxInactiveCol attribute represents the column in the sessions table that contains an integer representing the length of time that a session can remain inactive before becoming invalid.
sessionLastAccessCol	The sessionLastAccessCol attribute represents the column in the sessions table that contains the last time the session was accessed.
checkInterval	The checkInterval attribute represents the time in seconds in which Tomcat will check for and remove invalid sessions. If this interval is too short, Tomcat's performance can decrease significantly.
debug	The debug attribute represents the debug level for this JDBC store. The possible range is 0 to 99. The lowest value (0) means that no debug information is logged. You will probably want to set this value to 0 in a production environment.

Again, to see the effects of this change, you need to restart Tomcat and use the SessionServlet. After you have added a few attributes to the HttpSession, start the MySQL client as described in the "Creating the Sessions Database" section and enter the following two commands:

```
use tomcatsessions;
select id from sessions;
```

You should see a list of all the session identifiers currently in the store. That is all there is to it. Your session object will now be stored and retrieved, based upon the <Manager> settings, from the tomcatsessions database.

Summary

In this chapter, we discussed HTTP sessions and how they are used. After we had an understanding of HTTP sessions, we discussed how Tomcat could be configured to persist HTTP session objects to a database. In the next chapter, we cover Tomcat valves and servlet filters.

CHAPTER 8

Valves and Servlet Filters

IN THIS CHAPTER, we

- Discuss Tomcat valves and the valves included with Tomcat
- Describe servlet filters and how they are deployed

In this chapter, we discuss two similar technologies. The first, Tomcat valves, is a proprietary technology introduced in Tomcat 4, and the second, servlet filters, is a server-independent technology introduced with the new servlet specification 2.3. Both of these technologies are used to process HTTP request and response objects.

What is a Tomcat Valve?

A Tomcat valve—a new technology introduced with Tomcat 4—allows you to associate an instance of a Java class with a particular Catalina container. This configuration allows the named class to act as a preprocessor of each request. These classes are called *valves*, and they must implement the `org.apache.catalina.Valve` interface or extend the `org.apache.catalina.valves.ValveBase` class. Valves are proprietary to Tomcat and cannot, at this time, be used in a different servlet/JSP container.

Table 8-1 lists the Catalina containers that can host a Tomcat valve and the associated effect of this hosting.

NOTE *The available Catalina containers are described in Chapter 1.*

Table 8-1. The Containers That Can Host a Tomcat Valve

DIRECTORY	DESCRIPTION
`Engine`	A valve contained by a Catalina engine preprocesses all requests received by any `Connector` associated with the engine it is nested in.
`Host`	A valve contained by a Catalina host preprocesses all requests targeted to a particular virtual host.
`Context`	A valve contained by a particular Catalina context preprocesses all requests referencing the named context.

At this writing, Tomcat comes configured with four valves:

- Access Log
- Remote Address Filter
- Remote Host Filter
- Request Dumper

Each of these valves (and their available attributes) are described in the following sections.

NOTE *All Tomcat valves use the* `className` *attribute to denote the fully qualified class name of the object that implements the* `org.apache.catalina.Valve` *interface.*

The Access Log Valve

The first of the Tomcat prepackaged valves is the Access Log valve: `org.apache.catalina.valves.AccessLogValve`. It creates log files to track client access information. Some of the content that it tracks includes page hit counts, user session activity, user authentication information, and much more. The Access Log valve can be associated with an engine, host, or context container. The Access Log valve leverages the attributes described in Table 8-2.

Table 8-2. The Access Log Valve Attributes

ATTRIBUTE	DESCRIPTION
directory	The directory attribute references the relative or absolute pathname of the directory into which log files will be created. If an absolute path is not specified, the path is interpreted as relative to <CATALINA_HOME>. If no directory is specified, the default value is logs, which creates the log files in the logs directory relative to <CATALINA_HOME>.
pattern	The pattern attribute defines a formatting layout that identifies the various information fields that will be logged from the request and response. (Table 8-3 contains the possible pattern values.)
prefix	The prefix attribute names the text that will be prepended to the front of each log file name. If not specified, the default value is "access_log."
resolveHosts	The resolveHosts attribute determines if the IP address of the remote client should be resolved to its corresponding host name. If not specified, the default value is false, indicating that remote host resolution will not take place. You should consider setting this value to false in a production environment to improve Tomcat performance.
suffix	The suffix attribute names the text that will be appended to the end of each log file name. If a value is not specified, no suffix is appended to the file name.
timestamp	The timestamp attribute, if set to true, states that log messages will be date/time stamped. The default value is false (log messages will not be date/time stamped). You should consider setting this value to false in a production environment to improve Tomcat performance.

The following code snippet is an example entry using the org.apache.catalina.valves.AccessLogValve:

```
<Valve className="org.apache.catalina.valves.AccessLogValve"
  directory="logs"  prefix="localhost_access_log." suffix=".txt"
  pattern="common"/>
```

This code snippet states that the log files will be placed in the <CATALINA_HOME>/logs directory, prepended with the value localhost_access_log., and appended with the .txt suffix.

Table 8-3. The Available `pattern` *Attribute Values*

PATTERN ATTRIBUTE	DESCRIPTION
%a	The remote IP address
%A	The local IP address
%b	The number of bytes sent, excluding HTTP headers, or '-' if zero
%B	The number of bytes sent, excluding HTTP headers
%h	The remote host name, or the IP address if `resolveHosts` is false
%H	The request protocol
%l	The remote logical username from `identd` , which seems to always return -
%m	The request method (that is, GET, POST, and so on)
%p	The local port on which this request was received
%q	The query string prepended with a ?
%r	The first line of the request method and request URI
%s	The HTTP status code of the response sent to the client
%t	The date and time of the request and response
%u	The authenticated remote user, if any; otherwise - is logged
%U	The requested URL path
&v	The name of the local server

If you specify a pattern of `common` or do not specify a pattern at all, the `common` pattern `%h %l %u %t "%r" %s %b` is used.

The Remote Address Filter

The Remote Address filter, `org.apache.catalina.valves.RemoteAddrValve`, allows you to compare the IP address of the requesting client against one or more `regular` expressions to either allow or prevent the request from continuing based on the results of this comparison. A Remote Address filter can be associated with a Tomcat Engine, Host, or Context container. The Remote Address filter supports additional attributes, as listed in Table 8-4.

Table 8-4. The Remote Address Filter Valve Attributes

ATTRIBUTE	DESCRIPTION
allow	The allow attribute takes a comma-delimited list of regular expressions used to compare the remote IP address of the client. If this attribute is included, the remote address of the client must match at least one of the patterns to be allowed access. If this attribute is not specified, all requests are allowed, unless the remote address matches a deny pattern.
deny	The deny attribute acts as the inverse of the allow attribute: it denies access based upon a matched pattern of remote IP addresses.

The following code snippet is an example entry using the org.apache.catalina.valves.RemoteAddrValve.

```
<Valve className="org.apache.catalina.valves.RemoteAddrValve"
  deny="127.*"/>
```

This valve entry denies access to the assigned container for all client IP addresses that begin with 127. If I assign this valve entry to the host container localhost, then all clients with an IP address beginning with 127 will see a screen similar to that shown in Figure 8-1 when trying to access the localhost.

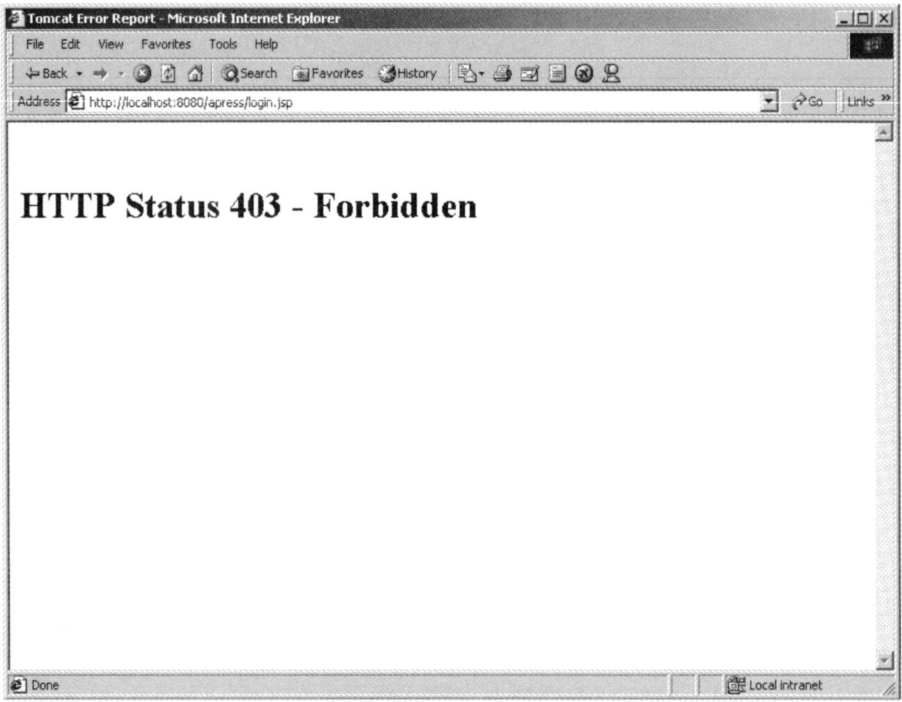

Figure 8-1. The `Deny` *response from the* `RemoteAddrValve`

The Remote Host Filter

The Remote Host filter—`org.apache.catalina.valves.RemoteHostValve`—is much like the `RemoteAddrValve`, except it allows you to compare the remote host address of the client that submitted this request instead of the fixed IP address. A Remote Host filter can be associated with a Tomcat Engine, Host, or Context container. The Remote Address Host supports the following additional attributes described in Table 8-5.

Table 8-5. The Remote Host Filter Valve Attributes

ATTRIBUTE	DESCRIPTION
`allow`	The `allow` attribute takes a comma-delimited list of regular expressions used to compare the remote hostname of the client. If this attribute is included, the remote address of the client must match at least one of the patterns to be allowed access. If this attribute is not specified, all requests are allowed unless the remote address matches a deny pattern.
`deny`	The `deny` attribute acts as the inverse of the `allow` attribute: it denies access based upon a matched pattern of remote hostnames.

An example entry using the org.apache.catalina.valves.RemoteHostValve can be found in the following code snippet.

```
<Valve className="org.apache.catalina.valves.RemoteHostValve"
  deny="virtuas*"/>
```

This valve entry denies access to the assigned container for all client hostnames including virtuas. If I assign this valve entry to the host container localhost, then all clients beginning with virtuas will see a screen similar to that shown Figure 8-1 when trying to access the localhost.

The Request Dumper Valve

The Request Dumper valve—org.apache.catalina.valves.RequestDumperValve—is a debugging tool that allows you to dump the HTTP headers associated with the specified request and response to the logger that is associated with our corresponding container. This valve is especially useful when you are trying to resolve any problems associated with headers or cookies sent by an HTTP client.
A Request Dumper filter can be associated with an Engine, Host, or Context container. The Request Dumper filter supports no additional attributes. An example entry using the org.apache.catalina.valve.RequestDumperValve can be found in the following code snippet:

```
<Valve className="org.apache.catalina.valves.RequestDumperValve"/>
```

To use the RequestDumperValve, you simply need to add this entry to the Tomcat container that you would like to monitor. To see this valve in action, open the current <TOMCAT_HOME>/conf/server.xml, uncomment the previously listed line found in the Standalone engine, and restart Tomcat. Now make a request to any of the applications found at http://localhost:8080. After the request has been processed, open the latest <TOMCAT_HOME>/logs/catalina_log file. You should see several entries made by the RequestDumperValve. These entries describe the contents of the most recent request.

NOTE *Do not leave this Valve enabled when in a production system. The amount of file IO produced by this Valve will slow Tomcat's response time considerably.*

What is a Servlet Filter?

Filters are a new feature introduced by the Java servlet specification version 2.3. They provide the necessary functionality to examine and transform the header information of both the request and response objects of a servlet container. Filters do not actually create the request and response object; they just modify them. Some characteristics of servlet filters are:

- Servlet filters can examine and modify both the `ServletRequest` and `ServletResponse` objects.
- Servlet filters are mapped to particular URL patterns of a Web application and won't be executed unless the URL mapping they are deployed to is requested.
- Servlet filters are part of the Java servlet specification version 2.3. Therefore, they are portable to all 2.3-compliant servlet containers.
- Autonomous servlet filters can be chained together to create a pipeline-type effect for modifying request and response objects.

To create your own servlet filter, you must create a class that implements the `javax.servlet.Filter` interface. Your filter class must also include a "no argument" public constructor. An example filter is shown in Listing 8-1.

Listing 8-1. `ExampleFilter.java`

```
package chapter8;

import java.io.IOException;
import javax.servlet.Filter;
import javax.servlet.FilterChain;
import javax.servlet.FilterConfig;
import javax.servlet.ServletContext;
import javax.servlet.ServletException;
import javax.servlet.ServletRequest;
import javax.servlet.ServletResponse;

public final class ExampleFilter implements Filter {

  public void init(FilterConfig config)
    throws javax.servlet.ServletException {
```

```
    System.err.println("---->ExampleFilter: INSIDE INIT<----");
  }

  public void destroy() {

    System.err.println("---->ExampleFilter: INSIDE DESTROY<----");
  }

  public void doFilter(ServletRequest request,
    ServletResponse response,
    FilterChain chain)
    throws java.io.IOException, javax.servlet.ServletException {

    System.err.println("---->ExampleFilter: Before doFilter()<----");

    request.setAttribute("logo",
      new String("/apress/images/monitor2.gif"));

    chain.doFilter(request, response);

    System.err.println("---->ExampleFilter: After doFilter()<----");
  }
}
```

As you examine `ExampleFilter`, you'll notice three distinct methods: `init()`, `destroy()`, and `doFilter()`. Each of these methods is defined by the `javax.servlet.Filter` interface and must be implemented by all servlet filter classes. These three methods form the lifecycle of methods of all servlet filters.

NOTE *The filter lifecycle methods have been named with the intention of having a similar nomenclature as the servlet lifecycle methods.*

The first of these methods, `init()`, is executed once for every instance of the servlet filter. It is much like the `init()` method defined by a servlet in that it should allocate all of the resources that will be used over the life of the filter. It takes a single parameter with a type of `javax.servlet.FilterConfig`, which provides access to initialization parameters and the `javax.servlet.ServletConfig` object.

NOTE *Filter initialization parameters are configured in the deployment descriptor,* `web.xml` *file, of the Web application hosting the servlet filter.*

Our `init()` method simply writes a simple text message to the error stream, allowing us to watch the life of the filter in the console from which Tomcat was executed.

The next method implemented by `ExampleFilter` is the `destroy()` method. This is where the life of the filter ends and all of its allocated resources must be reclaimed. In `ExampleFilter`, we are again simply printing some text to the error stream, allowing us to monitor the end of the filter's life.

The final method implemented by `ExampleFilter` is the `doFilter()` method. This method is executed with every request matching the URL pattern that it is deployed to. It is synonymous with the `service()` method of a Java servlet. The `doFilter()` method accepts three parameters: a `javax.servlet.ServletRequest`, a `javax.servlet.ServletResponse`, and a `javax.servlet.FilterChain`. The `ServletRequest` and `ServletResponse` objects are the objects that are actually being manipulated by the servlet filter, and the `FilterChain` object allows the filter to pass control of the request and response on to the next filter (if one exists).

In our `doFilter()` method, we are again printing some text to the error stream allowing us to monitor the processing of requests mapped to this filter. We then modify the request by adding an attribute named `logo` to the `ServletRequest` object. This attribute is the key of a string that represents the image to include on our `login.jsp` screen. We then pass control of the current request to the next filter in the chain (if there is one) by calling the `FilterChain.doFilter()` method. (We discuss chaining filters in a later section.) After all processing is complete, the processing is returned to this filter and then sent back to the client. This functionality it shown by the final action of the `Example.doFilter()` method, which is to print a message to the standard error stream showing that control has returned to this filter.

Deploying a Servlet Filter

To deploy `ExampleFilter`, we need to add two entries to the `apress web.xml` file. Our modified `web.xml` file can be found in Listing 8-2.

Listing 8-2. The Modified `web.xml` *File*

```
<?xml version="1.0" encoding="ISO-8859-1"?>
```

```
<!DOCTYPE web-app
    PUBLIC "-//Sun Microsystems, Inc.//DTD Web Application 2.3//EN"
    "http://java.sun.com/j2ee/dtds/web-app_2_3.dtd">

<web-app>

  <filter>
    <filter-name>Filter 1</filter-name>
    <filter-class>chapter8.ExampleFilter</filter-class>
  </filter>

  <filter-mapping>
    <filter-name>Filter 1</filter-name>
    <url-pattern>*.jsp</url-pattern>
  </filter-mapping>

  <servlet>
    <servlet-name>login</servlet-name>
    <servlet-class>chapter2.login</servlet-class>
  </servlet>

  <taglib>
    <taglib-uri>/apress</taglib-uri>
    <taglib-location>/WEB-INF/lib/taglib.tld</taglib-location>
  </taglib>

  <!-- Define a Security Constraint on this Application -->
  <security-constraint>
    <web-resource-collection>
      <web-resource-name>Apress Application</web-resource-name>
      <url-pattern>/*</url-pattern>
    </web-resource-collection>
    <auth-constraint>
      <role-name>apressuser</role-name>
      </auth-constraint>
  </security-constraint>

  <!-- Define the Login Configuration for this Application -->
    <login-config>
      <auth-method>BASIC</auth-method>
      <realm-name>Apress Application</realm-name>
    </login-config>
 </web-app>
```

The first of these entries, the <filter> element, defines the servlet filter itself using the sub-elements described in Table 8-6.

Table 8-6. The <filter> Sub-Elements

SUB-ELEMENT	DESCRIPTION
<filter-name>	This is the string that is used to uniquely identify the servlet filter. It is used in the <filter-mapping> sub-element to identify the filter to be executed, when a defined URL pattern is requested.
<filter-class>	This sub-element names the fully qualified filter class to be executed when the string defined in the <filter-name> sub-element is referenced in the <filter-mapping> element.

NOTE *Filter definitions must be defined prior to any servlet definitions in the* web.xml *file.*

The second of these two entries, the <filter-mapping> element, describes the servlet filter to execute and the URL pattern that must be requested to execute the filter. The sub-elements of this element are described in Table 8-7.

Table 8-7. The <filter-mapping> Sub-Elements

SUB-ELEMENT	DESCRIPTION
<filter-name>	This string names the servlet filter to execute when the defined URL pattern is requested.
<url-pattern>	This sub-element defines the URL pattern that must be requested to execute the named servlet filter. In this example, we are using the value *.jsp; therefore, all JSP requests will be processed by this filter.

NOTE *Make sure that the* <filter-name> *sub-element matches in both the* <filter> *and* <filter-mapping> *elements. This is the link between these two elements.*

To see ExampleFilter in action, you need to complete the following steps:

1. Build the chapter8.ExampleFilter class.
2. Copy the compiled class file into the <TOMCAT_HOME>/webapps/apress/WEB-INF/classes/chapter8/ directory.
3. Modify the apress web.xml file according to the changes found in Listing 8-2, making sure that the elements are added in the order of their appearance.
4. Change the login.jsp file to get the image location from the request attribute logo, as shown in Listing 8-3.
5. Restart the Tomcat Server.

Listing 8-3. The Modifed login.jsp

```
<html>
<head>
  <title>Apress Demo</title>
  <meta http-equiv="Content-Type" content="text/html; charset=iso-8859-1">
</head>

<body bgcolor="#FFFFFF" onLoad="document.loginForm.username.focus()">

  <table width="500" border="0" cellspacing="0" cellpadding="0">
    <tr>
      <td> </td>
    </tr>
    <tr>
    <td>
      <img src="<%=request.getAttribute("logo") %>"></td>
    </tr>
    <tr>
      <td> </td>
    </tr>
  </table>
```

```
    <table width="500" border="0" cellspacing="0" cellpadding="0">
      <tr>
        <td>
          <table width="500" border="0" cellspacing="0" cellpadding="0">
            <form name="loginForm" method="post" action="servlet/chapter2.login">
            <tr>
              <td width="401"><div align="right">User Name: </div></td>
              <td width="399"><input type="text" name="username"></td>
            </tr>
            <tr>
              <td width="401"><div align="right">Password: </div></td>
              <td width="399"><input type="password" name="password"></td>
            </tr>
            <tr>
              <td width="401"> </td>
              <td width="399"><br><input type="Submit" name="Submit"></td>
            </tr>
            </form>
          </table>
        </td>
      </tr>
    </table>
  </body>
  </html>
```

As the Tomcat server starts, watch the output of the console. You should see the standard error statements from the `init()` method. Now open you browser to the following URL:

```
http://localhost:8080/apress/login.jsp
```

If everything was changed correctly, you should see an image similar to that shown in Figure 8-2.

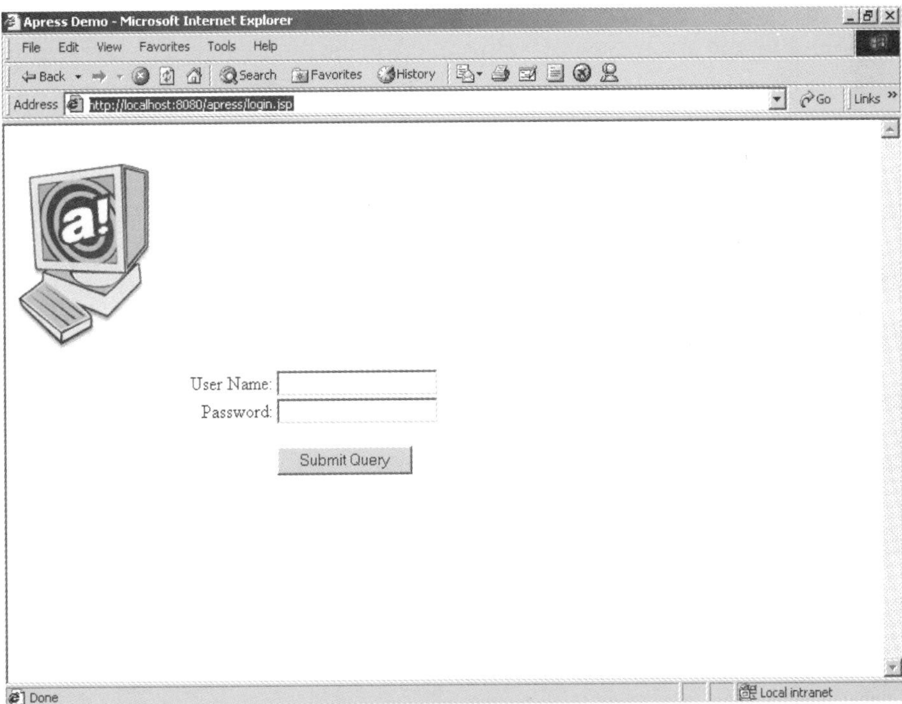

Figure 8-2. The `apress login.jsp` *with image from* `chapter8.ExampleFilter`

Now go back and examine the console window again. You should see an image similar to Figure 8-3 with the standard error statements from the `doFilter()` method.

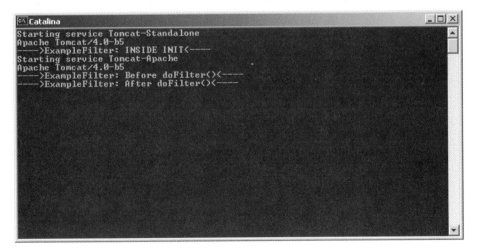

Figure 8-3. The standard error output from `doFilter()`

Although this filter was very simple, you could use a similar filter to look up a user profile and assign the logo value based on the profile values. This would give an application some simple personalization functionality.

Chaining Servlet Filters

Now that you have seen a filter change the incoming request, let's take a look at chaining a filter that will change the response object sent back to the client. The source code for the filter that we will chain is shown in Listing 8-4.

Listing 8-4. ExampleFilter2.java

```
package chapter8;

import javax.servlet.Filter;
import javax.servlet.ServletRequest;
import javax.servlet.ServletResponse;
import javax.servlet.FilterChain;
import javax.servlet.FilterConfig;
import java.io.PrintWriter;

public class ExampleFilter2 implements Filter {

  public ExampleFilter2() {

  }

  public void init(FilterConfig config)
    throws javax.servlet.ServletException {

    System.err.println("---->ExampleFilter2: INSIDE INIT<----");
  }

  public void destroy() {

    System.err.println("---->ExampleFilter2: INSIDE DESTROY<----");
  }

  public void doFilter(ServletRequest request,
    ServletResponse response,
    FilterChain chain)
    throws java.io.IOException, javax.servlet.ServletException {
```

```
    System.err.println("---->ExampleFilter2: Before doFilter()<----");
    chain.doFilter(request, response);
    System.err.println("---->ExampleFilter2: After doFilter()<----");

    PrintWriter out = response.getWriter();
    out.write("\n<!--Created by the Apress Application -->\n");
  }
}
```

As you examine the source code for ExampleFilter2, you'll notice that it contains very few changes. The first changes exist in the messages written to standard error. These changes simply add the number 2 to the standard messages, signifying the source of the statements.

The major change exists in the doFilter() method. In this method, we have added two lines, the first of which gets a reference to the PrintWriter contained in the ServletRequest. This PrintWriter contains the stream that will be written to the client's browser. Once we have this reference, we simply write an HTML comment string using the following line of code:

```
out.write("\n<!-- Created by the Apress Application -->\n");
```

The most important thing to note about this additional code is where the new statements exist: they are executed after the chain.doFilter() method is returned. This means that the login.jsp will have completed its execution, but the response will not go to the client browser until this filter has processed it. This makes it possible to add the comment to the bottom of the JSP output.

Deploying a Filter Chain

The steps involved in deploying a filter chain are much like deploying a single filter, with the exception of the following two rules:

- The <url-pattern> must match for all filters in the chain.
- The order in which the <filter-mapping> elements are defined determines the order in which they exist in the chain.

Listing 8-5 contains the modified web.xml with the appropriate changes to configure our filter chain.

Listing 8-5. The Modified `web.xml` *Including a Filter Chain*

```
<?xml version="1.0" encoding="ISO-8859-1"?>

<!DOCTYPE web-app PUBLIC
  '-//Sun Microsystems, Inc.//DTD Web Application 2.3//EN'
  'http://java.sun.com/j2ee/dtds/web-app_2_3.dtd'>

<web-app>

    <filter>
    <filter-name>Filter 1</filter-name>
    <filter-class>chapter8.ExampleFilter</filter-class>
  </filter>

  <filter>
  <filter-name>Filter 2</filter-name>
  <filter-class>chapter8.ExampleFilter2</filter-class>
</filter>

<filter-mapping>
  <filter-name>Filter 1</filter-name>
  <url-pattern>*.jsp</url-pattern>
</filter-mapping>

<filter-mapping>
  <filter-name>Filter 2</filter-name>
  <url-pattern>*.jsp</url-pattern>
</filter-mapping>

<servlet>
  <servlet-name>login</servlet-name>
  <servlet-class>chapter2.login</servlet-class>
</servlet>

<taglib>
  <taglib-uri>/apress</taglib-uri>
  <taglib-location>/WEB-INF/lib/taglib.tld</taglib-location>
</taglib>

<!-- Define a Security Constraint on this Application -->
<security-constraint>
  <web-resource-collection>
```

```
    <web-resource-name>Apress Application</web-resource-name>
    <url-pattern>/*</url-pattern>
  </web-resource-collection>
  <auth-constraint>
    <role-name>apressuser</role-name>
  </auth-constraint>
  </security-constraint>

  <!-- Define the Login Configuration for this Application -->
    <login-config>
  <auth-method>BASIC</auth-method>
  <realm-name>Apress Application</realm-name>
    </login-config>

</web-app>
```

As you can see by examining Listing 8-5, we have added a second filter definition that satisfies the previous two rules. It does this by defining the same `<url-pattern>` as the first filter and by defining a `<filter-mapping>` definition that follows the first filter's `<filter-mapping>` definition, which makes it second in the chain.

To complete the deployment of this filter chain, follow the deployment steps defined in the previous section ("Deploying a Servlet Filter"), substituting `ExampleFilter2` where appropriate. As the Tomcat server restarts, watch the output of the console. You should see the standard error statements from the `init()` methods of both the `ExampleFilter` and the `ExampleFilter2`. Now open your browser to the following URL:

```
http://localhost:8080/apress/login.jsp
```

If everything was changed correctly, your browser should display an image similar to the one shown in Figure 8-1. To see the change to the HTML source sent to the client, select the view source option for your particular browser and scroll to the bottom of the page. The following HTML comment should be listed on the very last line:

```
<!-- Created by the Apress Application -->
```

You should also examine the console output to confirm the order in which each filter is processed. That is all there is to it. Now this text will be added to every JSP request that exists in the `/apress` web application.

Summary

In this chapter, we discussed using both Tomcat valves and servlet filters. We described the valves included with Tomcat. We briefly introduced servlet filters and how they are deployed, and we also discussed how filters can be chained together. If you would like to learn more about servlet filters, you should take a look at the Java servlet specification version 2.3, which can be found at `http://www.javasoft.com`. In the next chapter, we cover integrating Tomcat and the Apache Web server.

CHAPTER 9

Integrating the Apache HTTP Server

IN THIS CHAPTER, we

- Describe the Apache Web server
- Integrate the Apache Web server and Tomcat

In this chapter, we cover the Apache HTTP Server Project. We also describe the steps required when integrating the Apache server into Tomcat.

What is the Apache Web Server?

The Apache Web Server Project is a collaborative open source development effort with the explicit goal of creating a commercial-quality HTTP server. The original code was based upon the `httpd 1.3` product developed by Rob McCool at the National Center for Supercomputing Applications (NCSA). The project began in February 1995 and was made publicly available in April 1995, with a 0.6.2 release.

The Apache server is a jointly supervised product, managed by a group of volunteers known as the Apache Group. This group is located around the world, using the Internet to correspond, plan, design, and develop the application. The Apache Group is also augmented by the open source community, which has contributed invaluable time and effort to the server's development. To complete the steps in this chapter, you need to download the Apache Web server, version 1.3x, from the following URL:

```
http://httpd.apache.org/dist/httpd/
```

Make sure you have the appropriate version for your operating system and then proceed with the installation, following the packaged instruction set. After you have completed the installation, make sure the Apache server is started and open your browser to the following URL:

```
http://localhost/
```

You should see the Apache Web server's test page, as shown in Figure 9.1.

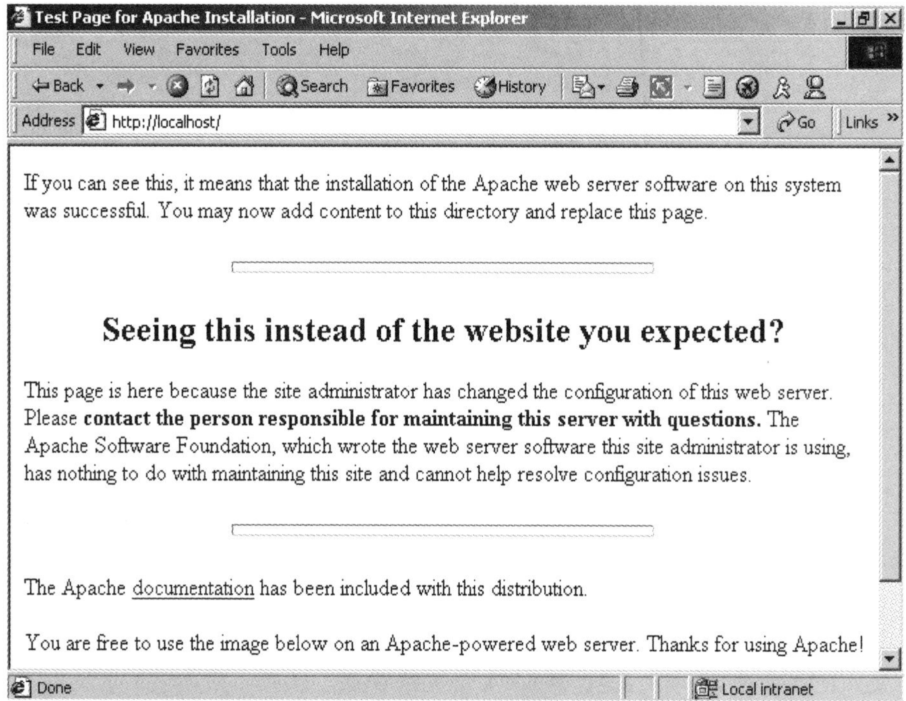

Figure 9-1. The test page for the Apache installation

Integrating Tomcat and the Apache Web Server

Tomcat uses an interface, called `org.apache.catalina.Connector`, to receive requests and return responses to a client application. This interface is extended to provide specialized connector classes that can receive requests and return responses to particular clients. Two connectors are packaged with Tomcat. The first, the HTTP connector, services basic HTTP requests. The second, the Warp connector, handles requests from other alternate clients. We'll use the Warp Connector to integrate to the Apache Web server. The implementation of this specialized class can be found in `org.apache.catalina.connector.warp.WarpConnector`.

Before we can begin to use the Warp connector, we need the Apache Web server component that talks to it. This component is implemented in an Apache module called the Web Application Module, and you can find it at:

```
http://jakarta.apache.org/builds/jakarta-tomcat-4.0/release/
```

Find the latest release of Tomcat and choose the `/bin` directory. You should see a list of Web application modules. Select the module that matches your release of Tomcat and download the archive. Once you have the appropriate release, extract the archive to your local disk. You should have a directory containing a file named `mod_webapp.so` and, if you are installing on any Windows OS, a file named `libapr.dll`.

NOTE *As of this writing, the Windows binary is still at beta 7. You can find this binary at* `http://www.apache.org/dist/jakarta/jakarta-tomcat-4.0/release/v4.0-b7/bin/`.

Now that we have all of the necessary components, we can begin our integration of Tomcat and the Apache Web server. The first step is to copy the `mod_webapp.so` file, found in the Web Application Module archive, into the Apache `/libexec` if installing to Linux, or the Apache `/modules` directory if you are performing a Windows installation. These directories are listed in Table 9-1.

Table 9-1. The Apache Modules Directories

OPERATING SYSTEM	DIRECTORY
Linux	<APACHE_HOME>/libexec
Windows NT/2000	<APACHE_HOME>/modules

If you are using Apache 1.3 for Windows, copy the `libapr.dll` file (which is also found in the Web Application Module archive) to the `<APACHE_HOME>/modules/` directory. If you do not perform this step, the Apache server will not start, reporting that the Web application module cannot be loaded.

Once you have copied the appropriate files to the appropriate locations, edit the Apache `httpd.conf` file, found in the `<APACHE_HOME>/conf/` directory, by adding the following lines for a Linux installation:

```
LoadModule webapp_module libexec/mod_webapp.so
AddModule mod_webapp.c
```

or the following lines if you are installing to Windows:

```
LoadModule webapp_module modules/mod_webapp.so
AddModule mod_webapp.c
```

NOTE *A logical place for these two entries is at the end of all of the commented-out* `LoadModule` *directives and at the end of all of the commented-out* `AddModule` *directives, respectively.*

Now it's time to add the proper entries to publish your Web application connections and context paths to Apache. To do this, for the `/examples` Web application, add the following lines to the end of the `<APACHE_HOME>/conf/httpd.conf` file:

```
WebAppConnection conn warp localhost:8008
WebAppDeploy examples conn /examples
```

The first line of this entry adds a Warp connection to a Tomcat server running on the `localhost` and listening to `port` 8008, for all incoming requests. The format of this entry is:

```
WebAppConnection connectionname provider host:port
```

The attributes of this entry are described in Table 9-2.

Table 9-2. The Attributes of the `WebAppConnection` *Entry*

COMPONENT	DESCRIPTION
`connectionname`	Represents the unique name for the connection to be created between Apache and Tomcat
`provider`	Represents the name of the provider used to connect to the servlet container. The Warp connector is currently the only provider available.
`host:port`	Identifies the host name and port number to which the Warp connection will try to connect. The `host` part of this entry must match the name of the server where Tomcat is running, and the `port` must match the `port` attribute of the Warp connector defined in the `server.xml` file. We define the Warp connector later in this chapter.

The second line of this entry defines a Web application that is associated with the previously defined connection. In this entry, we are defining the Web application named `examples` that is associated with the connection `conn` and has a context path of `/examples`. The format of this entry is as follows:

```
WebAppDeploy applicationname connectionname path
```

The attributes of this entry are described in Table 9-3.

Table 9-3. The Attributes of the `WebAppDeploy` *Entry*

COMPONENT	DESCRIPTION
`applicationname`	The name of a Web application that is present in the Tomcat `webapps` directory
`connectionname`	Names the connection of a previously declared `WebAppConnection`
`path`	Names the path element of the URL where this application will be deployed

The next step in this process is to define a new Tomcat service to handle Apache Web server requests. To do this, we need to add the following code snippet to the top-level `<Server>` element of the `<TOMCAT_HOME>conf/server.xml` file. If this element already exists, you can skip this step.

```
<!-- Define an Apache-Connector Service -->
<Service name="Tomcat-Apache">

  <Connector className="org.apache.catalina.connector.warp.WarpConnector"
   port="8008" minProcessors="5" maxProcessors="75"
   enableLookups="true"
   acceptCount="10" debug="0"/>

  <!-- Replace "localhost" with what your Apache "ServerName" is set to -->
  <Engine className="org.apache.catalina.connector.warp.WarpEngine"
   name="Apache" debug="0" appBase="webapps">


    <!-- Global logger unless overridden at lower levels -->
    <Logger className="org.apache.catalina.logger.FileLogger"
            prefix="apache_log." suffix=".txt"
            timestamp="true"/>

    <!-- Because this Realm is here, an instance will be shared globally -->
    <Realm className="org.apache.catalina.realm.MemoryRealm" />

  </Engine>

</Service>
```

This entry defines a new service that will handle all requests from the Apache Web server. This service contains some default elements, but the significant items to note are the `className` and `port` attributes of the `<Connector>` element. These elements state that this service uses a Warp connector and that this connector listens to port `8008`.

NOTE *If you want the Apache Web server to handle all HTTP requests for your Web applications, you may consider removing the default* `<Service>` *entry in the* `server.xml` *file. The default entry contains an HTTP connector that continues to service HTTP requests on port 8080 or 80 depending upon your initial installation.*

At this point, you have installed all of the appropriate Warp components, defined a Warp connection, and associated a Web application to the defined Warp connection. The next step is to test this integration. Start Tomcat, and then start the Apache Web server. Now open your browser to the following URL:

```
http://localhost/examples/
```

NOTE *If Apache does not start, try commenting out the* `AddModule` *directive that was added to the* `<APACHE_HOME>/conf/httpd.conf` *file. This is probably an issue only with the beta being used at the time of this writing and will most likely be resolved with the 4.0 release of Tomcat.*

You should see a page similar to that shown in Figure 9-2.

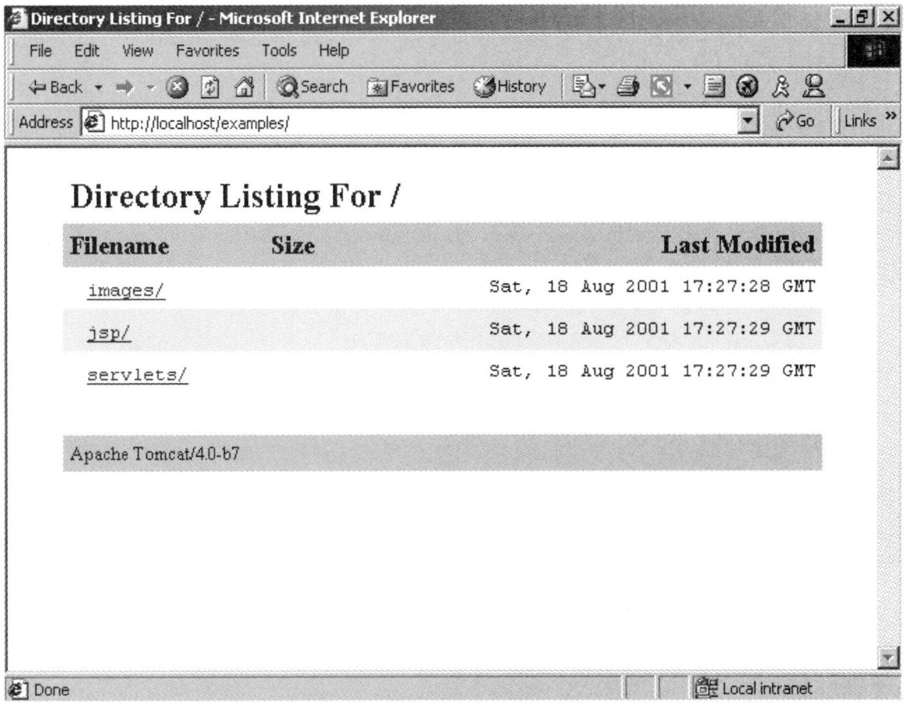

Figure 9-2. The directory listing for the `examples` *Web application*

NOTE *Make sure that your URL does not reference port 8080 and that it does include the trailing slash /. The Apache Web server uses the default HTTP port of 80, and the trailing slash must be included, because there are no files in the root directory of the* `examples` *Web application.*

That's about it. You should now be able to browse around in the `examples` Web application, without any trouble. If you want to add the `apress` Web application, add the following line after the `examples WebAppDeploy` entry in the `<APACHE_HOME>/conf/httpd.conf` file:

```
WebAppDeploy apress conn /apress
```

Summary

In this chapter, we discussed the Apache Web server. We described each of the steps involved when integrating the Apache server with the Tomcat container. We then completed the chapter by describing the steps required when adding Web applications to the Apache/Tomcat integration. In the next chapter, we discuss how the Apache Jakarta Struts project can be integrated into Tomcat.

CHAPTER 10

Integrating the Jakarta-Struts Project

IN THIS CHAPTER, we

- Describe the Jakarta-Struts Project
- Create and install a Struts Web application
- Step through the actions of a Struts Web application

In this chapter, we describe the Jakarta-Struts Project and how it can be used. We discuss the steps involved when creating and installing a Struts application, using Tomcat. We conclude the chapter with a walk-through of the actions being performed in our example Struts Web application.

The Jakarta-Struts Project

The Jakarta-Struts Project (Struts) is an open source project sponsored by the Apache Software Foundation. It is a server-side, Java model-view-controller (MVC) framework that Craig McClanahan created sometime in May of 2000. The Struts project was fashioned with the intent of providing an open source framework for creating Web applications that would leverage both the Java servlets and JavaServer pages technologies. Since its inception, Struts has received quite a bit of developer support and is quickly becoming a dominant player in the open source community.

Understanding the MVC Design Pattern

As stated earlier, the Struts framework is based on the MVC (Model 2) design pattern, which originated from Smalltalk and was used to design graphical user interfaces. MVC applications comprise three classes: model, view, and controller. Each is defined in Table 10-1.

Table 10-1. The Three Components of the MVC Model

COMPONENT	DESCRIPTION
Model	The model component represents the data objects. The model is what is being manipulated and presented to the user.
View	The view component is the screen representation of the model. It is the object that presents the current state of the data objects.
Controller	The controller component defines the way that the user interface reacts to the user's input. The controller component is the object that manipulates the model or data object.

The major advantage of using the MVC design pattern is that it separates the view and the model, making it possible to separate presentation from business logic, which in turn allows you to create or change the view without having to change model or controller functionality.

The Struts Implementation of the MVC

The Struts framework implements a server-side implementation of the MVC pattern via a combination of JSPs, custom JSP tags, and Java servlets. In this section, we briefly discuss how the Struts framework maps to each component of the MVC. When we have completed this discussion, we will have drawn a picture similar to Figure 10-1.

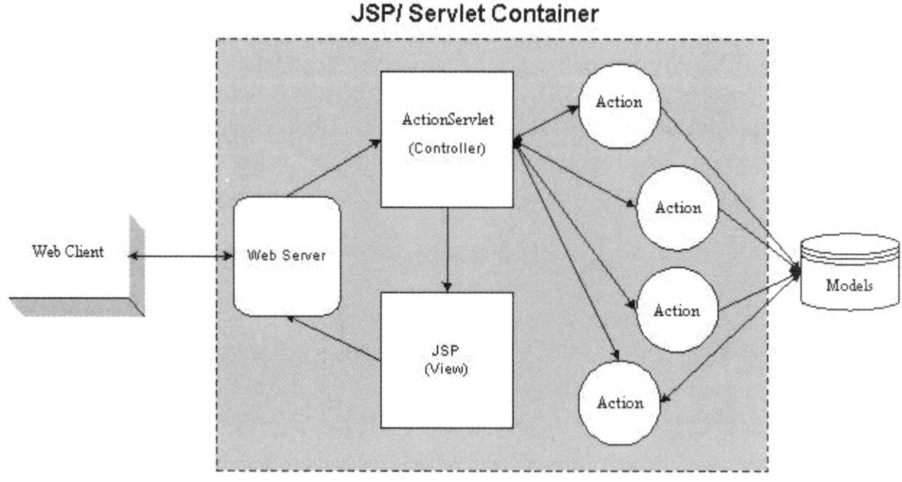

Figure 10-1. The Struts framework maps well to the MVC model.

The Model

The Struts framework is not packaged with model components. The model components are defined as custom application business logic and are created by the implementer of a Struts solution.

The View

The view components of the Struts framework include a JSP for each view and any combination of Struts custom tags. An example Struts view can be found in the following code snippet:

```
<%@page language="java">
<%@taglib uri="/WEB-INF/struts-html.tld" prefix="html">
<html:form action="loginAction.do"
  name="loginForm"
  type="chapter10.loginForm" >

  User Id: <html:text property="username"><br/>
  Password: <html:password property="password"><br/>
  <html:submit />
</html:form>
```

We will build a working Struts view in the example application discussed at the end of this chapter.

The Controller

The controller component of the Struts framework is the backbone of all Struts Web applications. It is implemented as a servlet, `ActionServlet`, that receives requests from a client and delegates control of the request to a user-defined `Action` class. The `ActionServlet` delegates control based upon the URI of the incoming request. The `ActionServlet` is similar to a factory that creates `Action` objects.

Creating and Installing a Struts Web Application

Now that you have a high-level understanding of the Struts framework, let's create and install our own Struts application. To do this, we need to download the following list of items:

- The latest **Jakarta-Struts** binary for your operating system. For these examples, I am using Struts 1.0, which can be found at `http://jakarta.apache.org`.
- The latest **Xerces Java Parser**. I am using Xerces 1.3, which can be found at `http://xml.apache.org`.

After you have gathered these two items, we can begin the development of a simple Struts example. To do this, you first must complete the following steps:

1. Uncompress the Struts archive to your local disk.
2. Copy the `struts-blank.war` file, found in the `webapps` directory of the Struts directory, to the `webapps` directory of your Tomcat installation.

NOTE *The* `struts-blank.war` *file is a Struts Web archive that contains the basic components of all Struts Web applications. It provides you with a baseline for developing your own Struts applications.*

3. Rename the `struts-blank.war` file to `apress-struts.war`.
4. Restart Tomcat. Once Tomcat starts, you should see a new directory named `apress-struts`.
5. Uncompress the Xerces archive to you local disk.
6. Copy the `xerces.jar` file from the Xerces root directory to the `<TOMCAT_HOME>/webapps/apress-struts/WEB-INF/lib/` directory.

NOTE *If you plan to deploy several Struts applications to a single instance of Tomcat, you can replace the target directory (in step 6) with the* `<TOMCAT_HOME>/lib/` *directory. This makes the* `xerces.jar` *file available to all of your Struts applications.*

7. Restart Tomcat and open your browser to the following URL:

```
http://localhost:8080/apress-struts/
```

NOTE *If you are starting Tomcat from a console, you'll see additional information being logged by the Struts application. This is normal and should not be considered erroneous.*

If everything went according to plan, you should see a page similar to that shown in Figure 10-2.

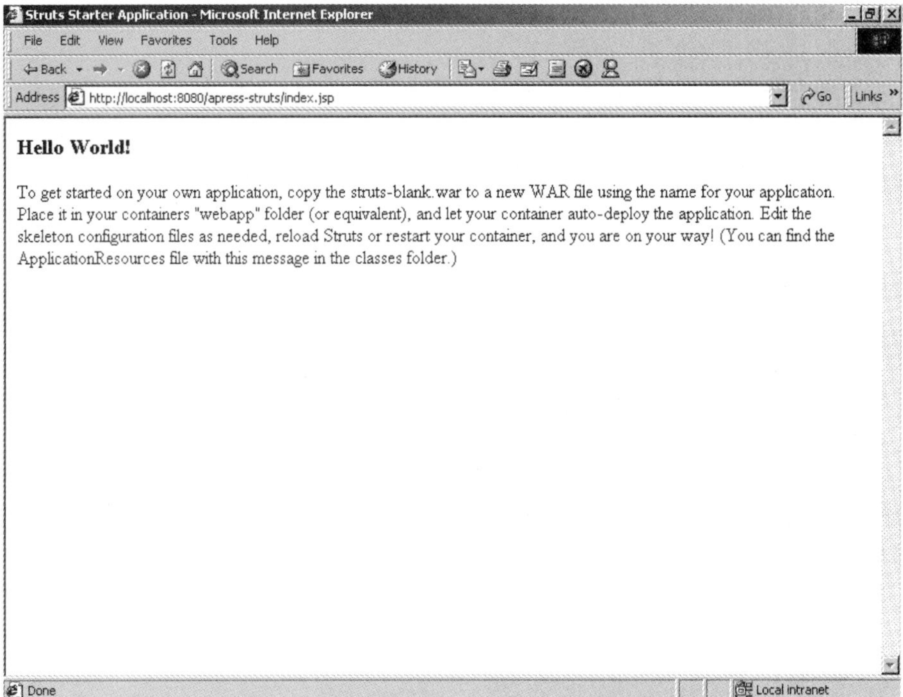
Struts Starter Application - Microsoft Internet Explorer
File Edit View Favorites Tools Help
Back Search Favorites History
Address http://localhost:8080/apress-struts/index.jsp
Go Links
Hello World!
To get started on your own application, copy the struts-blank.war to a new WAR file using the name for your application. Place it in your containers "webapp" folder (or equivalent), and let your container auto-deploy the application. Edit the skeleton configuration files as needed, reload Struts or restart your container, and you are on your way! (You can find the ApplicationResources file with this message in the classes folder.)
Done
Local intranet

Figure 10-2. The Struts starter page

Now we can begin developing our Struts example. For this example, we convert the `apress` Web application from Chapter 2 to a Struts application called `apress-struts`.

The Views

Several steps are necessary to convert our `apress` application. First, though, we'll describe the two views in our application and the changes that are required to convert both the `login.jsp` and `welcome.jsp`.

The Login View

The first of our views is `login.jsp`, which also is our starting view. Listing 10-1 reveals the changes we need to make to this JSP.

Listing 10-1. The Struts Version of `login.jsp`

```
<%@ taglib uri="/WEB-INF/struts-bean.tld" prefix="bean" %>
<%@ taglib uri="/WEB-INF/struts-html.tld" prefix="html" %>

<html>
<head>
  <title><bean:message key="app.title"/></title>
</head>

  <table width="500" border="0" cellspacing="0" cellpadding="0">
    <tr>
      <td> </td>
    </tr>
    <tr>
    <td>
      <img src="images/monitor2.gif"></td>
    </tr>
    <tr>
      <td> </td>
    </tr>
  </table>

  <html:form action="Login.do"
    name="loginForm"
    scope="request"
    type="chapter10.LoginForm" >
    <table width="45%" border="0">
      <tr>
        <td><bean:message key="app.username"/>:</td>
        <td><html:text property="username" /></td>
      </tr>
      <tr>
        <td><bean:message key="app.password"/>:</td>
        <td><html:password property="password" /></td>
      </tr>
      <tr>
        <td colspan="2" align="center"><html:submit /></td>
```

```
      </tr>
    </table>
  </html:form>

</body>
</html>
```

As you look over this file, notice the changes (in bold type) that have been made from the original `login.jsp`. The first change is the inclusion of two tag library directives, the first of which is the Struts Bean tags. The tags in this library will be used later for loading predefined text messages from a text file called a `ResourceBundle`. Loading text using this method allows you to swap languages by only changing files. The second included tag library contains HTML tags that are used to populate `ActionForm` objects that correspond to the form in this view.

The first real change is in the HTML `<title>` element. The original title text was static, while now it is being loaded from a `ResourceBundle` used by the `message` tag of the Bean library. This tag has a single attribute `key` that is used to look up the text that will be substituted for the tag text. The message tag is replaced by whatever value is referenced by the `key`. Three of these tags are used in this JSP, and their format is defined in the following code snippet:

```
<bean:message key="unique key"/>
```

The file that contains the text used by these tags is the `/<TOMCAT_HOME/apress-struts/WEB-INF/classes/ApplicationResources.properties` file. The contents of this file for our application can be found in Listing 10-2.

Listing 10-2. The Contents of the `ApplicationResource.properties` *File*

```
app.title=Apress Struts Application
app.username=User Name
app.password=Password
```

To make these messages available to this application, you need to delete the file's current values and replace them with the values in Listing 10-2.

The next section to look at is the Struts HTML `form` tag. This tag encapsulates Struts form processing and is the parent of all form tags. The `form` tag represents a standard HTML form. The `form` tag attributes used in this example are described in Table 10-2.

Table 10-2 The Attributes of the `form` Tag Used in This Example

COMPONENT	DESCRIPTION
`action`	The `action` attribute represents the URL to which this form is submitted. This attribute is also used to find the appropriate `ActionMapping` in the Struts configuration file, which we describe later in this section. The value used in our example is `Login.do`, which maps to an `ActionMapping` with a `path` attribute equal to `Login`.

NOTE *The `.do` appended to the `action` is used as part of a URL pattern that tells the Tomcat that all requests ending with `.do` should be serviced by the `ActionServlet`.*

COMPONENT	DESCRIPTION
`scope`	The `scope` attribute represents the scope within which the form bean associated with this input form will be accessed or created. The available options are either `request` or `session`. Our `ActionForm` is created and stored in the `request`.
`name`	The `name` attribute identifies the key that the `ActionForm` is referenced by. We use the value `loginForm`.
`type`	The `type` attribute names the fully qualified class name of the form bean to use in this request. For this example, we use the value `chapter10.LoginForm`, an `ActionForm` that contains attributes matching the inputs of this form.

The cumulative effect of these attributes states the following:

- Upon submission, we will execute the `Action` object with an `ActionMapping` containing a `path` equal to `Login`.
- The `ActionForm` object for this form will be stored in the request.
- The name by which the `ActionForm` will be referenced is `loginForm`.
- The fully qualified class path of the `ActionForm` is `chapter10.LoginForm`.

This instance of the `form` is also the parent to five tags, two Bean `message` tags (which we discussed earlier), and three tags from the HTML library. There is really nothing more to discuss about the `message` tags, but we do need to cover the three HTML tags: `<html:text>`, `<html:password>`, and `<html:submit>`.

The first two HTML tags—`<html:text>` and `<html:password>` tags—are synonymous with their HTML input counterparts. The difference, however, is in the `property` attribute, which names a unique attribute found in the `ActionForm` bean of this form. The named attribute is set to the `text` value of the input tag.

The last `html` tag we used is the `<html:submit>` tag, which simply emulates an HTML Submit button.

The Welcome View

The second of our views is the `welcome.jsp`. This view is the success target of the previous form. The changes we made to this JSP can be found in Listing 10-3.

Listing 10-3. The Struts Version of `welcome.jsp`

```
<%@ taglib uri="/WEB-INF/struts-bean.tld" prefix="bean" %>

<html>
<head>
  <title><bean:message key="app.title"/></title>
</head>

  <table width="500" border="0" cellspacing="0" cellpadding="0">
    <tr>
      <td> </td>
    </tr>
    <tr>
    <td>
      <img src="images/monitor2.gif"></td>
    <td>
      <b>Welcome : <%= request.getAttribute("USER") %></b>
    </td>
    </tr>
    <tr>
      <td> </td>
    </tr>
  </table>
</body>
</html>
```

As you look this JSP over, you may notice that it contains only minor changes from its original version. The two changes include the `taglib` directive identifying the `bean` tags and a single use of the `<bean:message>` tag used to dynamically load the `<title>` text.

The Model

In this example, we have only a single model object. This object is an implementation of ActionForm, which contains attributes that map directly to the input parameters of the form defined in the Login view. The source code for our ActionForm is shown in Listing 10-4.

Listing 10-4. Our ActionForm *Implementation* LoginForm.java

```
package chapter10;

import javax.servlet.http.HttpServletRequest;
import org.apache.struts.action.ActionForm;
import org.apache.struts.action.ActionMapping;

public class LoginForm extends ActionForm {

  private String password = null;

  private String username = null;

  // Password Accessors
  public String getPassword() {

    return (this.password);
  }

  public void setPassword(String password) {

    this.password = password;
  }

  // Username Accessors
  public String getUsername() {

    return (this.username);
  }

  public void setUsername(String username) {

    this.username = username;
  }
```

```
  // This method is called with every request. It resets the Form
  // attribute prior to setting the values in the new request.
  public void reset(ActionMapping mapping, HttpServletRequest request) {

    this.password = null;
    this.username = null;
  }
}
```

There is nothing special about this class: it is a simple bean that extends `org.apache.struts.action.ActionForm` with get and set accessors for each of its attributes. However, it does have one method that is specific to an `ActionForm` bean—the `reset()` method—which is called with each request using the `LoginForm` resetting all of its attributes.

To deploy the `LoginForm` to our Struts application, you need to compile this class, move it to the `<TOMCAT_HOME>webapps/apress-struts/WEB-INF/classes/chapter10` directory, and add the following line to the `<form-beans>` section of the `<TOMCAT_HOME>webapps/apress-struts/WEB-INF/struts-config.xml` file:

```
<form-bean name="loginForm" type="chapter10.LoginForm"/>
```

This entry makes the Struts application aware of the `LoginForm` and how it should be referenced.

NOTE *The* `struts-config.xml` *file is the deployment descriptor for Struts applications. Think of this file as the glue that binds all of the MVC components together.*

The Controller

The final piece of our Struts application is the controller. For this component, we are going to create a Struts `Action` bean named `LoginAction` that contains the same basic functionality as the `login.java` servlet found in the `apress` Web application. The source for our `Action` bean can be found in Listing 10-5.

Listing 10-5. The `LoginAction` *Bean*

```
package chapter10;

import java.io.IOException;
import javax.servlet.ServletException;
```

```
import javax.servlet.http.HttpServletRequest;
import javax.servlet.http.HttpServletResponse;
import org.apache.struts.action.Action;
import org.apache.struts.action.ActionForm;
import org.apache.struts.action.ActionForward;
import org.apache.struts.action.ActionMapping;

public class LoginAction extends Action {

  protected String getUser(String username, String password) {

    String user = null;

    // You would normally do some real User lookup here, but
    // for this example we will have only one valid username "bob"
    System.err.println(username + ":" + password);
    if ( username.equals("bob") && password.equals("password") ) {

      user = new String("Bob");
    }
    return user;
  }

  public ActionForward perform(ActionMapping mapping,
    ActionForm form,
    HttpServletRequest request,
    HttpServletResponse response)
    throws IOException, ServletException {

    String user = null;

    // Default target to success
    String target = new String("success");

    // Use the LoginForm to get the request parameters
    String username = ((LoginForm)form).getUsername();
    String password = ((LoginForm)form).getPassword();

    user = getUser(username, password);

    // Set the target to failure
    if ( user == null ) {
```

```
        target = new String("failure");
      }
      else {

        request.setAttribute("USER", user);
      }
      // Forward to the appropriate View
      return (mapping.findForward(target));
    }
  }
```

The main functionality of the `LoginAction` is found in the `perform()` method. This is the method that must be defined by all `Action` classes that are invoked by the controller. To understand how the `perform()` method works, we first examine the four parameters passed to the `perform()` method and then discuss the actual method body. These parameters are described in Table 10-3.

Table 10-3. The Parameters of the `Action.perform()` *Method*

COMPONENT	DESCRIPTION
ActionMapping	The `ActionMapping` class contains all of the deployment information for a particular `Action` bean. This class will be used to determine the physical target of this `LoginAction` later in the method.
ActionForm	The `ActionForm` represents the model object containing the request parameters from the view referencing this `Action` bean.
HttpServletRequest	The `HttpServletRequest` attribute is simply a reference to the current HTTP request object.
HttpServletResponse	The `HttpServletResponse` is simply a reference to the current HTTP response object.

Now that we have described the parameters passed to the `perform()` method, we can move on to describing the actual method body. The first notable action taken by this method is to create a `String` object named `target` with a value of `success`. This object will be used to determine the view that will present the results of this `Action`. For this example, we have set the default to be a successful transaction.

NOTE *The value of the* `target` *object is used to look up the view JSP that this request will be forwarded to, once the* `perform()` *method has completed its processing. The target values are described in an* `<action>` *element in the* `struts-config.xml`, *which is described later in this section.*

The next step performed by this method is to get the request parameters contained in the `LoginForm`. When the form was submitted, the `ActionServlet` used Java's reflection mechanism to set the values stored in this object. The following code snippet displays the source code used to access the request parameters:

```
// Use the LoginForm to get the request parameters
String username = ((LoginForm)form).getUsername();
String password = ((LoginForm)form).getPassword();
```

Once we have references to the username and password parameters, we pass these values to the `getUser()` method. This method is a simple user-defined method that returns the `String Bob` if the username and password equal `bob` and `password`, respectively. If the `username` and `password` contain any other values, `null` is returned and we change the value of our `target` to `failure`. This has the effect of changing the targeted view. If `Bob` was returned from `getUser()`, then we add `Bob` to the `request` with a key of `USER`.

At this point, the value of `target` equals either `success` or `failure`. This value is then passed to the `ActionMapping.findForward()` method, which returns an `ActionForward` object containing the physical view that will actually present the results of this `Action`. The final step of the `perform()` method is to return the `ActionForward` object to the invoking `ActionServlet`, which then forwards the `request` to the contained view for presentation. This step is completed using the following line of code:

```
return (mapping.findForward(target));
```

To deploy the `LoginAction` to our Struts application, you need to compile this class, move it to the `<TOMCAT_HOME>webapps/apress-struts/WEB-INF/classes/chapter10` directory, and add the following entry to the `<action-mappings>` section of the `<TOMCAT_HOME>webapps/apress-struts/WEB-INF/struts-config.xml` file:

```
<action path="/Login"  type="chapter10.LoginAction" name="loginForm" >
  <forward name="success" path="/welcome.jsp"/>
  <forward name="failure" path="/index.jsp"/>
</action>
```

This entry contains the data that will be stored in the `ActionMapping` object that is passed to the `perform()` method of the `LoginAction`. It contains all of the attributes required to use this instance of the `LoginAction`, including a collection of keyed `<forward>` sub-elements that represent the possible views that can present the results of the `LoginAction`.

Walking Through the *apress-struts* Web Application

By this point, you should have completed all of the steps described in the previous section and have a deployed `apress-struts` Web application. We are now going to go through this example application and discuss each of the steps performed by Struts along the way.

To begin using this application, you need to restart Tomcat and open your Web browser to the following URL:

```
http://localhost:8080/apress-struts/login.jsp
```

If everything went according to plan, you should see a page similar to that shown in Figure 10-3.

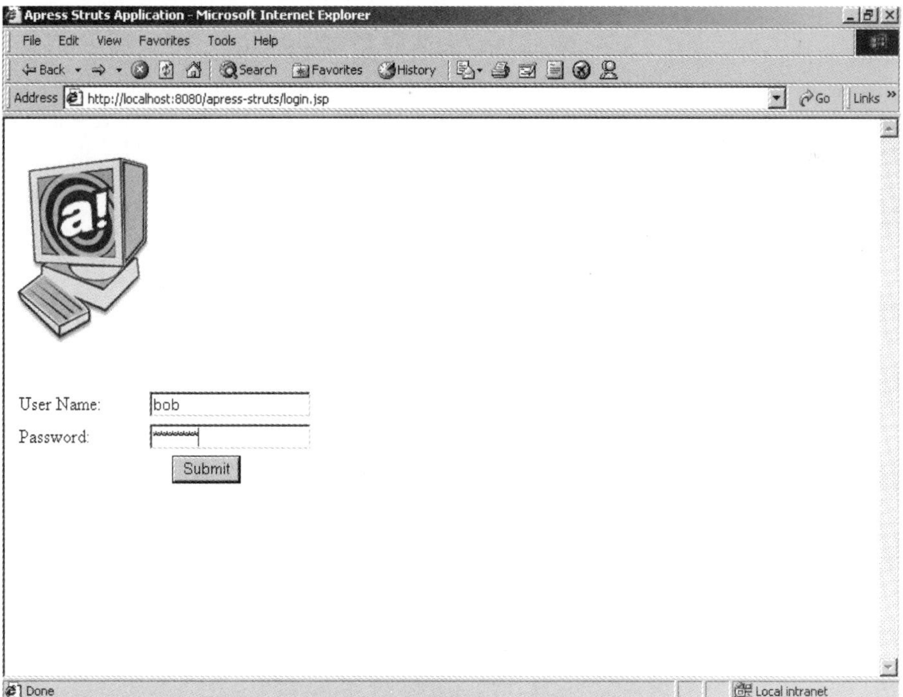

Figure 10-3. The `apress-struts` *Login view*

When this page was loaded the following actions occurred:

1. The `<bean:message>` custom tags loaded the text resources from the `/<TOMCAT_HOME/apress-struts/WEB-INF/classes/ApplicationResources.properties` file and replaced the tag text with the appropriate values.

2. The `<html:form>` bean checked for an instance of the `chapter10.LoginForm` that exists in `request` scope. If there were an instance, the values will be mapped to the input elements values on the form.

3. The Login view is then presented to the user.

You should now go ahead and enter the values `bob` and `password` into the appropriate text boxes and click on the Submit button. This invokes the following functionality:

1. The servlet/JSP container looks in the `web.xml` file for a `<servlet-mapping>` with a `<url-pattern>` that ends with `do`. It will find the following entry, which tells the container to send the request to a servlet that has been deployed with a `<servlet-name>` of `action`.

```
<!-- Standard Action Servlet Mapping -->
<servlet-mapping>
  <servlet-name>action</servlet-name>
  <url-pattern>*.do</url-pattern>
</servlet-mapping>
```

2. The container will find the following `<servlet>` entry with a `<servlet-name>` of `action` that points to the `ActionServlet`, which acts as the controller for all Struts applications.

```
<servlet>
  <servlet-name>action</servlet-name>
  <servlet-class>org.apache.struts.action.ActionServlet</servlet-class>
</servlet>
```

NOTE *I have removed some of the* `<servlet>` *sub-elements for simplicity.*

3. The ActionServlet then takes over the servicing of this request by creating an instance of the LoginForm and populating its attributes with the values passed on the request and adding the LoginForm to the request with a key of loginForm.

4. At this point, the ActionServlet looks for an <ActionMapping> entry in the struts-config.xml file with a <path> element equal to Login. It finds the following entry:

```
<action path="/Login"
  type="chapter10.LoginAction"
  name="loginForm" >
  <forward name="success" path="/welcome.jsp"/>
  <forward name="failure" path="/index.jsp"/>
</action>
```

5. It then creates an instance of the LoginAction class (if one does not already exist) named by the type attribute and an ActionMapping class containing all of the values in the <ActionMapping> element. It then invokes the LoginAction.perform() with the appropriate parameters.

6. The LoginAction.perform() method performs its logic and calls the ActionMapping.findForward() method with a String value of success.

7. The ActionMapping.findForward() method looks for a <forward> sub-element with a name attribute that matches success. It then returns an ActionForward object containing the results of the lookup, which is the value of the path attribute /welcome.jsp.

8. The LoginAction then returns the ActionForward object to the ActionServlet, which in turn forwards the request object to the targeted view, /welcome.jsp, for presentation.

9. The Welcome view then uses a <bean:message> custom tags lookup and displays the HTML <Title> and presents the results of the LoginAction, which should look similar to that shown in Figure 10-4.

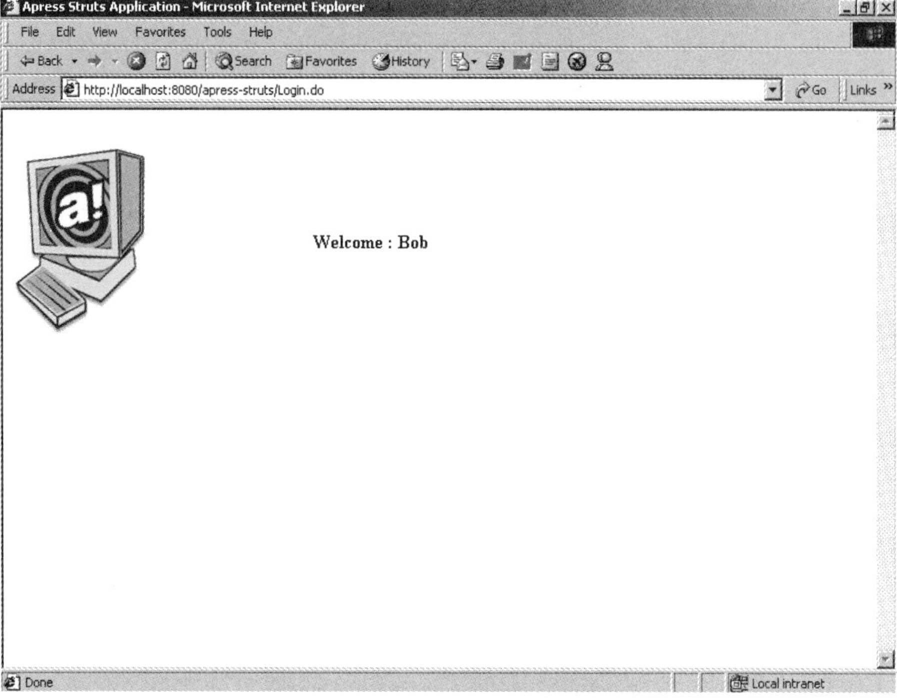

Figure 10-4. The `apress-struts` *Welcome view*

Summary

In this chapter, we discussed the Apache-Jakarta Project's Struts. We defined the framework and its uses, and we described the Struts components. We also went through a working example of developing and deploying a Struts Web application, using Tomcat. However, we only scratched the surface of this project. If you are interested in further information about the Struts framework, you can find it at the Struts Web site: `http://jakarta.apache.org/struts/index.html`. In the next chapter, we discuss how the Jakarta Log4J Project can be integrated into Tomcat.

CHAPTER 11

Integrating the Jakarta-Log4J Project

IN THIS CHAPTER, we

- Describe the Jakarta-Log4J project
- Use Log4J in an application
- Integrate Log4J into a Web application

In this chapter, we cover the Jakarta-Log4J project and how it can be used. We also describe how you can use Log4J in a normal Java application. We conclude this chapter with an example of how you can leverage Log4J in a Web application, using Tomcat.

The Jakarta-Log4J Project

The Jakarta-Log4j project (Log4J) is another open source project sponsored by the Apache Software Foundation. It was founded by Ceki Gulcu with the intention of providing application developers with a sophisticated—yet simple—logging mechanism that could be integrated into Java applications. The Log4J project comprises three main components: `Layouts`, `Appenders`, and `Categories`. We describe each of these components in the following sections. To follow the examples in this chapter, you need the latest archive of log4j, which can be found at `http://jakarta.apache.org/log4j/`.

Layouts

`Layouts` allow you to customize the output format of a Log4J message. They must be assigned to `Appenders`, which are discussed in the following section. The simplest of the Log4J `Layouts` is the `SimpleLayout`, which logs only the `Priority` and the message. To assign the SimpleLayout to an Appender, we could use something similar to the following code snippet:

```
log4j.appender.console.layout=org.apache.log4j.SimpleLayout
```

This line assigns a SimpleLayout to a previously defined Appender named console. We discuss the appropriate location of Layout assignments in a subsequent section on configurators. Output using the SimpleLayout would look similar to the following:

```
DEBUG - This is the log message!
```

You can find further documentation on the other Layouts packaged with Log4J.

Appenders

Appenders allow logging requests to be printed to multiple output destinations such as consoles, files, NT event loggers, and many others.

The most common way to leverage an Appender is to assign it a Layout and then assign it to a Category. This is done using a code snippet similar to the following:

```
log4j.category.chapter11.Log4JApp= DEBUG, console
log4j.appender.console=org.apache.log4j.ConsoleAppender
log4j.appender.console.layout=org.apache.log4j.SimpleLayout
```

As you examine the previous snippet, you should ignore the first line. (It is discussed in the following section.) We need to focus on the second and third lines of this snippet. The second line defines an Appender named console that uses the org.apache.log4j.ConsoleAppender, which does just as it sounds and logs all messages to the application console.

The third line of this snippet assigns the Layout class org.apache.log4j.SimpleLayout to the console Appender. These lines together define an Appender named console that outputs all of its messages in the format defined by the SimpleLayout object to the application console. In the next section, we close the loop by assigning the Appender to a Category.

Categories

Categories are the heart of Log4J. They allow developers to define how and when a log statement should be executed and then assign this definition a case-sensitive name that it can be referenced by. This name is the `Category` name that can be loaded and used to log messages. An example of this would be a `Category` that logged all "debug" statements to the `Appender` defined in the previous section. An example definition of a `Category` doing just this is contained in the following code snippet:

```
log4j.category.chapter11.Log4JApp= DEBUG, console
```

This statement defines a `Category` named `chapter11.Log4JApp` that logs all messages with a priority of `DEBUG` or higher to the console of the running application. The `DEBUG` and `console` values associated with this `Category` define the priority level of this `Category` and the name of the `Appender` to use when logging a message, respectively. `Categories` are referenced by name, and so to access the previous `Category` definition you would call the static `Category.getInstance()` method with the name of the `Category`:

```
static Category cat = Category.getInstance("chapter11.Log4JApp");
```

This statement creates an instance of a `Category` that can be used to log messages based on the previous `Category` definition. You can now log messages using any of the logging methods described in the next section.

NOTE *All* `Category` *definitions must be prepended with the string* `log4j.category`.

Priorities

`Priorities` are assigned to `Categories` to determine which log messages to actually log. The set of possible priorities are `DEBUG`, `INFO`, `WARN`, `ERROR`, and `FATAL`.

If a category is not assigned a priority, it inherits its category from its closest ancestor with an assigned priority. A `Category` must contain a `Priority` level, either explicitly, by naming the `Priority` in the `Category` definition, or implicitly, through inheritance.

Messages are logged based upon their priority. This is done using the `Category's` logging methods: `debug()`, `info()`, `warn()`, `error()`, and `fatal()`, which map one-to-one with the defined `Priorities` described previously. So, if you wanted to log a message with a priority of `DEBUG`, you would execute something similar to the following:

```
cat.debug("This is the DEBUG log message!");
```

This statement logs a message to the Category referenced by cat with Priority level of DEBUG. To determine whether the message is actually logged, the Category must examine its defined Priority. In this instance, the message is logged because the assigned Category Priority, DEBUG, is less than or equal to the Priority used in the debug() method. The Priority order is defined as follows:

```
DEBUG < INFO < WARN < ERROR < FATAL
```

Configurators

Now that we know how the three main components of Log4J are used, we can take a look at how these components are configured for actual use. Log4J can be configured programmatically or by using configuration files. For our examples, we use configuration files.

NOTE *The previous examples of configuring Log4J* Layouts, Appenders, *and* Categories *used a properties format, which is also used in Log4J's configuration files.*

Log4J currently supports two types of configuration files: a regular Java properties file and an XML properties file. We will use a Java properties file for our examples.

A Log4J properties file can be divided into three sections. Each section maps to a Category, an Appender, or a Layout. The following code snippet contains a sample properties file.

```
## CATEGORIES ##
#define a category named chapter11.Log4JApp
log4j.category.chapter11.Log4JApp=WARN, console, file

## APPENDERS ##
# define an appender named console, which is set to be a ConsoleAppender
log4j.appender.console=org.apache.log4j.ConsoleAppender

# define an appender named file, which is set to be a RollingFileAppender
log4j.appender.file=org.apache.log4j.RollingFileAppender
log4j.appender.file.File=log.txt
```

```
## LAYOUTS ##
# assign a layout to both appenders
log4j.appender.console.layout=org.apache.log4j.SimpleLayout
log4j.appender.file.layout=org.apache.log4j.SimpleLayout
```

The best way to examine this file is to start from the top with the `CATEGORIES` section. In this section, we define a new `Category` named `chapter11.Log4JApp`. In its definition, we are setting the log `Priority` to `WARN`. We are also assigning two `Appenders` to this `Category`, `console` and `file`, which are both defined in the `APPENDERS` section.

The next section is the `APPENDERS` section, which defines the available `Appenders` for this configuration. Here, we define two `Appenders`: `console` and `file`. The `console Appender` uses the `ConsoleAppender` class that we spoke of earlier, which simply logs all messages to the application console. The `file Appender` uses the `RollingFileAppender`, which appends all of the log messages to a log file named by the `log4j.appender.file.File` property.

The final section of this file is the `LAYOUTS` section. In this section, we are directing both the `console` and `file Appenders` to use the `SimpleLayout`, which is represented by `org.apache.log4j.SimpleLayout`.

In summary, this configuration file defines a `Category` named `chapter11.Log4JApp` that logs all messages with a `Priority` that is greater than or equal to `WARN` to both the console and a file named `log.txt` in a format similar to the following:

```
DEBUG - This is the log message!
```

To load this configuration, you would use the static `PropertyConfigurator.configure()` method with the path to the Log4J properties file. The following line of code gives an example of this.

```
PropertyConfigurator.configure(propfile);
```

Category Hierarchies

If a category's `Priority` and `Appender` are not explicitly defined, the hierarchy of the categories determines its `Priority` and `Appender`. `Category` hierarchies are very similar to Java packaging, whereas a category named `chapter11.Log4JApp` would be a parent of a category named `chapter11.Log4JApp.child`. An example configuration file with a parent/child relationship can be found in Listing 11-1.

Listing 11-1. A Simple Log4J Properties File `properties.lcf`

```
## CATEGORIES ##
#define a category named chapter11.Log4JApp
log4j.category.chapter11.Log4JApp=WARN, file

#define a second category that is a child to chapter11.Log4JApp
log4j.category.chapter11.Log4JApp.child

## APPENDERS ##
# define an appender named console, which is set to be a ConsoleAppender
log4j.appender.console=org.apache.log4j.ConsoleAppender

# define an appender named file, which is set to be a RollingFileAppender
log4j.appender.file=org.apache.log4j.RollingFileAppender
log4j.appender.file.File=log.txt

## LAYOUTS ##
# assign a layout to both appenders
log4j.appender.console.layout=org.apache.log4j.SimpleLayout
log4j.appender.file.layout=org.apache.log4j.SimpleLayout
```

As you can see, the second `Category chapter11.Log4JApp.child` does not have an assigned `Priority` or `Appender`, but, because the second category is a child of the first, it inherits its parent's definition. We will see an example of this in the following section.

Using Log4J in an Application

Now that we have a basic understanding of Log4J and its components, let's actually look at how it can be used. We are going to do this by creating a standard Java application that loads a Log4J properties file and uses the defined categories to log its messages. The properties file that we are using can be found in Listing 11-1 in the previous section.

The source Java application that will use the properties file can be found in Listing 11-2.

Listing 11-2. A Simple Log4J Application `Log4JApp.java`

```
package chapter11;

import org.apache.log4j.Category;
import org.apache.log4j.Priority;
```

```
import org.apache.log4j.BasicConfigurator;
import org.apache.log4j.PropertyConfigurator;

public class Log4JApp {

  // Get an instance of the chapter11.Log4JApp Category
  static Category cat =
    Category.getInstance("chapter11.Log4JApp");
  // Get an instance of the chapter11.Log4JApp.child Category
  // which is a child of chapter11.Log4JApp
  static Category childcat =
    Category.getInstance("chapter11.Log4JApp.child");

  public static void main(String[] args) {

    // Load the properties using the PropertyConfigurator
    PropertyConfigurator.configure("properties.lcf");

    // Log Messages using the Parent Category
    cat.debug("This is a log message from the " +
      cat.getName());
    cat.info("This is a log message from the " +
      cat.getName());
    cat.warn("This is a log message from the " +
      cat.getName());
    cat.error("This is a log message from the " +
      cat.getName());
    cat.fatal("This is a log message from the " +
      cat.getName());

    // Log Messages using the Child Category
    childcat.debug("This is a log message from the " +
      childcat.getName());
    childcat.info("This is a log message from the " +
      childcat.getName());
    childcat.warn("This is a log message from the " +
      childcat.getName());
    childcat.error("This is a log message from the " +
      childcat.getName());
    childcat.fatal("This is a log message from the " +
      childcat.getName());
  }
}
```

There is really nothing special about this file: it starts by loading two categories `cat` and `childcat`, with the first being the parent, referencing the `chapter11.Log4JApp Category` definition, and the second referencing `chapter11.Log4JApp.child Category` definition, which is the child of the first.

After these two categories are loaded, we begin making log requests to them. For each `Category`, we are calling all of the priority-driven logging methods, passing them a simple message with the category name appended to the end. The result is a log file named `log.txt` that contains all of the log messages with a priority of `WARN` or greater. An example of this file after a single execution can be found in the following snippet:

```
WARN - This is a log message from the chapter11.Log4JApp
ERROR - This is a log message from the chapter11.Log4JApp
FATAL - This is a log message from the chapter11.Log4JApp
WARN - This is a log message from the chapter11.Log4JApp.child
ERROR - This is a log message from the chapter11.Log4JApp.child
FATAL - This is a log message from the chapter11.Log4JApp.child
```

As you look over this file, you should note that the `childcat` did in fact inherit the `cat's Priority` and `Appender`. To see this example run, make sure the `log4j.jar` from the Log4J distribution is in your CLASSPATH, compile the source from Listing 11-2, create a properties file with settings similar to Listing 11-1, and execute the following command:

```
java chapter11.Log4JApp
```

Integrating Log4J into the *apress* Web Application

In this, our final section of the chapter, we go though the process of integrating Log4J into a Web application running in Tomcat. Although the Tomcat portion of this integration is minimal, it is very important to know how you can integrate a logging mechanism like Log4J into your Web applications.

We can perform this integration in several ways, and the method we are going to use requires that we add a new servlet to our existing `apress` Web application that will load and initialize the Log4J properties upon startup. This provides all of the components existing in this `apress` Web application access to `Category` definitions, which in turn allows them to log messages to these categories. The source code for the servlet that performs this initialization can be found in Listing 11-3.

Listing 11-3. The Source Code of the Log4J Initializing Servlet `Log4JServlet.java`

```
package chapter11;

import javax.servlet.*;
import javax.servlet.http.*;
import java.io.*;
import java.util.*;

import org.apache.log4j.PropertyConfigurator;

public class Log4JServlet extends HttpServlet {

  public void init()
    throws ServletException {

    // Get Fully Qualified Path to Properties File
    String path = getServletContext().getRealPath("/");
    String propfile = path + getInitParameter("propfile");

    // Initialize Properties for All Servlets
    PropertyConfigurator.configure(propfile);
  }

  public void doGet(HttpServletRequest request,
    HttpServletResponse response)
    throws ServletException, IOException {

    PrintWriter out = response.getWriter();


    out.println("<html>");
    out.println("<head><title>Log4JServlet</title></head>");
    out.println("<body>");
    out.println("<p>The servlet has received a GET. This is the reply.</p>");
    out.println("</body></html>");
  }

  public void destroy() {

  }
}
```

The code that performs the initialization can be found in the servlet's init() method. In this method, we are first getting a reference to a string that contains the real path of the Web application, which in this case is <TOMCAT_HOME>/webapps/apress/. We are then getting a reference to the servlet initialization parameter, propfile, which contains the location of the Log4J properties file. To deploy this servlet, we must complete the following steps:

1. Copy the log4j.jar file into the <TOMCAT_HOME>/common/lib directory. This makes Log4J available to all applications running under this instance of Tomcat.

2. Add the following <servlet> definition to the apress web.xml file. This entry defines a single <init-parameter> that references the location of the properties file. It also states that this servlet should be loaded on starting the application.

```
<servlet>
    <servlet-name>log4J</servlet-name>
    <servlet-class>chapter11.Log4JServlet</servlet-class>
    <init-param>
      <param-name>propfile</param-name>
      <param-value>WEB-INF/log4j.properties</param-value>
    </init-param>
    <load-on-startup>1</load-on-startup>
  </servlet>
```

3. Create a properties file named log4j.properties containing the following definitions and copy it to the <TOMCAT_HOME>/webapps/apress/WEB-INF/ directory:

```
log4j.category.com.apress=DEBUG, file

# console is set to be a RollingFileAppender which outputs to named file
log4j.appender.file=org.apache.log4j.RollingFileAppender
log4j.appender.file.File=<TOMCAT_HOME>/webapps/apress/WEB-INF/log.txt

# file uses SimpleLayout
log4j.appender.file.layout=org.apache.log4j.SimpleLayout
```

NOTE *You need to change the* `<TOMCAT_HOME>` *reference in the properties file to match your installation.*

4. Compile the `Log4JServlet.java` servlet and move it into the `<TOMCAT_HOME>/webapps/apress/WEB-INF/classes/chapter11` directory.

5. Restart Tomcat.

That is all there is to it; your application now has access to the Log4J `Category` named `com.apress`. To access this `Category`, you simply need to add a call to `Category.getInstance()`, similar to the following, to any of your `apress` components. You also need to import the `org.apache.log4j.Category` package, which contains the `Category` classes.

```
Category cat = Category.getInstance("com.apress");
```

An example of this can be found in Listing 11-4, which contains the JSP `login.jsp` that has been modified to log the address of the remote user upon every request.

Listing 11-4. A Modified Version of `login.jsp` *Using Log4J*

```
<%@ page import="org.apache.log4j.Category" %>
<html>
<head>
  <title>Apress Demo</title>
  <meta http-equiv="Content-Type" content="text/html; charset=iso-8859-1">
</head>

<%

  Category cat = Category.getInstance("com.apress");
  cat.info("Receiving request from " + request.getRemoteAddr());

%>

<body bgcolor="#FFFFFF" onLoad="document.loginForm.username.focus()">

  <table width="500" border="0" cellspacing="0" cellpadding="0">
```

```
      <tr>
        <td> </td>
      </tr>
      <tr>
      <td>
        <img src="/apress/images/monitor2.gif"></td>
      </tr>
      <tr>
        <td> </td>
      </tr>
    </table>
    <table width="500" border="0" cellspacing="0" cellpadding="0">
      <tr>
        <td>
          <table width="500" border="0" cellspacing="0" cellpadding="0">
            <form name="loginForm" method="post" action="servlet/chapter2.login">
            <tr>
              <td width="401"><div align="right">User Name: </div></td>
              <td width="399"><input type="text" name="username"></td>
            </tr>
            <tr>
              <td width="401"><div align="right">Password: </div></td>
              <td width="399"><input type="password" name="password"></td>
            </tr>
            <tr>
              <td width="401"> </td>
              <td width="399"><br><input type="Submit" name="Submit"></td>
            </tr>
            </form>
          </table>
        </td>
      </tr>
    </table>
  </body>
  </html>
```

To see Log4J working in the apress application, point your browser to http://localhost:8080/apress/login.jsp. After you have made this request, you can open the <TOMCAT_HOME>/webapps/apress/WEB-INF/log.txt and see the results of these changes.

Summary

In this chapter, we discussed the Apache-Log4J project and each Log4J major component. We then integrated Log4J into a Java application, and we also went through the steps involved when integrating Log4J into a Web application, using Tomcat. You can find more about the Log4J Project on the Log4J homepage (`http://jakarta.apache.org/log4j/docs/index.html`). In the next chapter, we discuss how the XML Apache Soap project can be integrated into Tomcat.

CHAPTER 12

Integrating the Apache SOAP Project

IN THIS CHAPTER, we

- Describe the Apache SOAP Project
- Integrate SOAP into Tomcat
- Create a sample SOAP application

In this chapter, we describe the Apache SOAP project and how it is used. We also explore how the Apache SOAP project can be integrated into Tomcat, and we conclude with an example SOAP application that is hosted by Tomcat.

Introducing the Apache SOAP Project

The Apache SOAP project is an open source Java implementation of the Simple Object Access Protocol v1.1 (SOAP). SOAP is a wire protocol that leverages HTTP or SMTP as its transport layer and XML as its data layer to execute remote methods, known as *SOAP services*.

The Apache implementation of SOAP provides two methods for invoking SOAP services. The first, which is our topic of discussion in this chapter, is the Remote Procedure Call (RPC) method. The RPC method is a synchronous technique using a client-server model to execute remote SOAP services. This model can be defined using the following steps:

1. A client application builds an XML document containing the URI of the server that will service the request, the name of the method to execute on the server, and the parameters associated with the method.

2. The targeted server receives and unwinds the XML document. It then executes the named method.

3. After the named method has returned its results, the results are packed into a response XML document and then sent back to the calling client.

4. The client application receives the response and unwinds the results, which contains the response of the invocated method.

The second method of invoking SOAP services is a message-based model using SMTP to transport the SOAP documents to and from the appropriate SOAP server. Although this method is interesting, it is outside the scope of a book describing the Tomcat container. If you would like more information about SOAP, you can begin with the following list of SOAP resources:

- `http://www.webservices.org`
- `http://www.develop.com/soap`
- `http://www.ibm.com/developerworks/webservices`

Integrating Apache SOAP into Tomcat

Before we begin using the Apache SOAP project, we must acquire the necessary components to execute SOAP services. Table 12-1 provides a list of the necessary items and their locations.

Table 12-1. Components Required to Execute SOAP Clients and Services

COMPONENT	LOCATION
SOAP v2.2	`http://xml.apache.org/soap/index.html`
`crimson.jar`	This JAR file is packaged with Tomcat in the `<TOMCAT_HOME>/server/lib/` directory.
`jaxp.jar`	This JAR file is packaged with Tomcat in the `<TOMCAT_HOME>/server/lib/` directory.
`mail.jar` v1.2	`http://java.sun.com/products/javamail/`
`activation.jar` v1.0.1	`http://java.sun.com/products/javabeans/glasgow/jaf.html`
`xerces.jar` v1.4.2	`http://xml.apache.org/xerces-j/index.html`

Once we have all of these items, we need to extract the SOAP archive to a local directory. Then we need to add each of the previously mentioned JAR files to your CLASSPATH, including the `soap.jar`, which comes packaged with the SOAP archive. This step is very important and must not be ignored.

Deploying Apache-SOAP Using Tomcat

The easiest way to deploy a SOAP project to Tomcat is to use the sample SOAP application included in the archive that you downloaded in the previous section. To do this, copy the `soap.war` file, found in the SOAP `/webapps` directory, to the `<TOMCAT_HOME>/webapps/` directory. Then, copy each of the JAR files (from Table 12-1) except the `soap.jar` file into the `<TOMCAT_HOME>/common/lib/` directory.

After you have copied these files to the named locations, restart Tomcat. You should now be able to access the SOAP Web application, by opening your Web browser to the following URL:

```
http://localhost:8080/soap/
```

You should see a page similar to that shown in Figure 12-1.

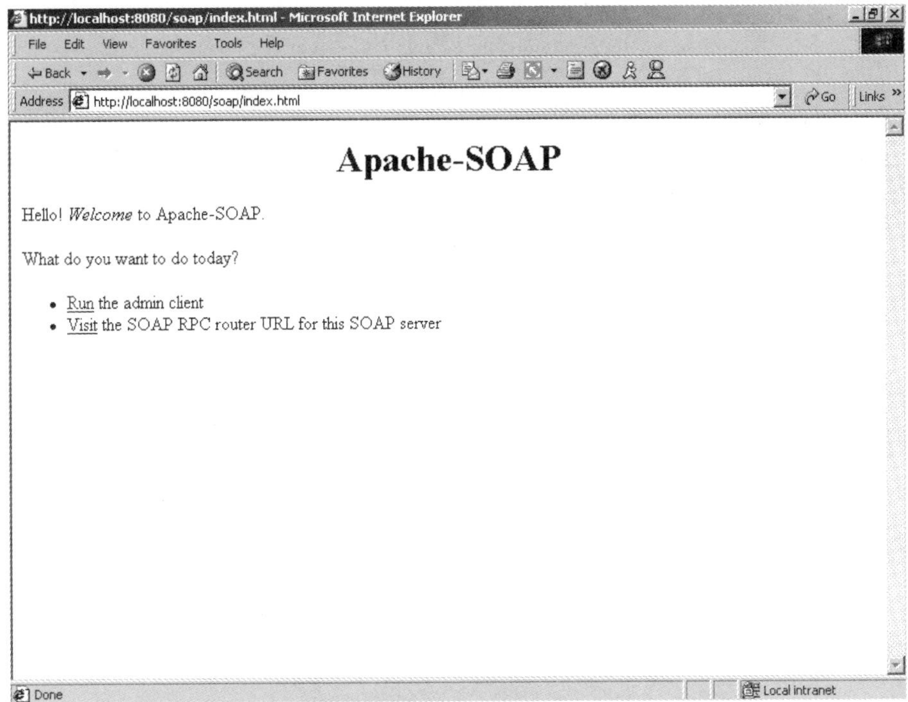

Figure 12-1. The SOAP application Welcome page

At this point, you should also be able to use the SOAP admin tool, which can be accessed by selecting the Run link. Figure 12-2 shows the homepage for the SOAP admin tool. From this page, you can list the current services, deploy new services and remove previously deployed services.

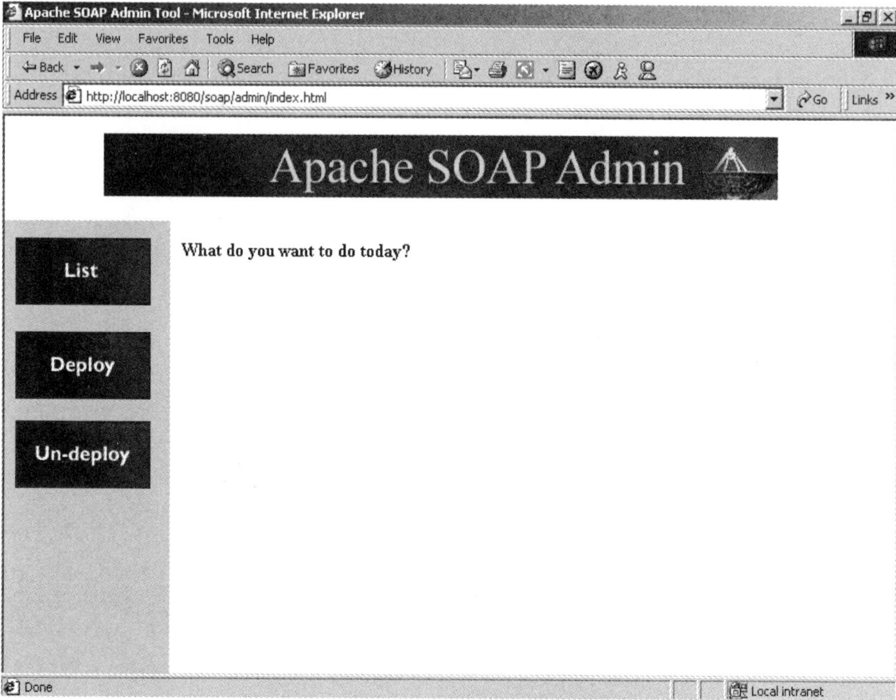

Figure 12-2. The SOAP Admin Tool homepage

Creating a Sample SOAP Application

In this section, we develop a simple SOAP application that acts as a limited calculator, with only addition and subtraction operations. We first develop a SOAP service for handling both our addition and subtraction methods, and then we create a client to access the services.

SOAP Services

Writing an RPC-based SOAP service is a very simple process that can be broken down into two steps: the first step is to create the Java class that contains the SOAP service that you wish to publish, and the second step is to create a deployment descriptor that describes this service. Each step is described in its own section.

Creating a SOAP Service

Creating a SOAP service is the simplest step of the entire "SOAPifying" process. A SOAP service can be just about any Java class that exposes public methods for invocation. The class does not need to know anything about SOAP or even that it is being executed as a SOAP service. The only restriction is that the method parameters be serializable. The available types that can, by default, be used by SOAP services are included in the SOAP registry. The following list contains the Java types included in the registry:

- all Java primitive types and their corresponding wrapper classes
- Java arrays
- `java.lang.String`
- `java.util.Date`
- `java.util.GregorianCalendar`
- `java.util.Vector`
- `java.util.Hashtable`
- `java.util.Map`
- `java.math.BigDecimal`
- `javax.mail.internet.MimeBodyPart`
- `java.io.InputStream`
- `javax.activation.DataSource`
- `javax.activation.DataHandler`
- `org.apache.soap.util.xml.QName`
- `org.apache.soap.rpc.Parameter`
- `java.lang.Object`

As mentioned earlier, our service is a simple calculator that is limited to addition and subtraction. This service can be found in Listing 12-1 in its entirety.

Listing 12-1. The Source Code for Our Limited Calculator `CalcService.java`

```
package chapter12;

public class CalcService {

  public int add(int p1, int p2) {

    return p1 + p2;
  }

  public int subtract(int p1, int p2) {

    return p1 - p2;
  }
}
```

As you can see, there is nothing special about this entire class: it simply defines two public methods—`add()` and `subtract()`—each with a parameter list containing two native `int`s. To make this class available to the `rpcrouter`, copy it into the `<TOMCAT_HOME>/webapps/soap/WEB-INF/classes/chapter12/` directory.

Creating the Deployment Descriptor

The second step to creating a new SOAP service is to create a deployment descriptor. The deployment descriptor describes the SOAP service, and this description is required for the service to be published to the Apache `rpcrouter`. The deployment descriptor for our service is contained in Listing 12-2.

Listing 12-2. The Calculator Deployment Descriptor `DeploymentDescriptor.xml`

```
<isd:service xmlns:isd="http://xml.apache.org/xml-soap/deployment"
             id="urn:apressserver">
  <isd:provider type="java"
                scope="application"
                methods="add subtract">
    <isd:java class="chapter12.CalcService"/>
  </isd:provider>
  <isd:faultListener>org.apache.soap.server.DOMFaultListener</isd:faultListener>
</isd:service>
```

The deployment descriptor for our calculator service contains only three elements that we need to look at: `service`, `provider`, and `java`. The first element, `service`, defines two attributes (the XML namespace and the unique `id` of the service to be deployed), and it is the parent of the entire deployed service.

NOTE *The* `id` *defined in the* `service` *element must be unique. This attribute is used, by the SOAP client, to look up a published SOAP service.*

The next element we need to examine is the `provider` element, which defines the actual implementation of the SOAP service. It does this with three attributes, each of which is defined in Table 12-2.

Table 12-2. The Three Attributes of the `provider` *Element*

COMPONENT	DESCRIPTION
`type`	The `type` attribute defines the implementation type of the SOAP service.
`scope`	The `scope` attribute defines the lifetime of the SOAP service. The possible values are `page`, `scope`, `session`, and `application`. These `scope` values map one-to-one with the `scope` values defined by the JSP specification that we discussed in Chapter 3.
`methods`	The `methods` attribute defines the names of the method that can be invoked on this service object. This list should be a space-separated list of method names.

The final element of the deployment descriptor is the `java` element. This element contains a single attribute, `class`, which names the fully qualified class that implements the named service.

Running the Server-Side Admin Tool to Manage Services

After you have compiled your service and moved it into the Web application CLASSPATH, you need to deploy it as a SOAP service. The Apache SOAP project is packaged with two administration tools, one graphical and one command-line. Both allow you to easily deploy and undeploy services to the SOAP server. The three functions provided by each of these tools are listed below:

- The deploy function allows you to deploy a new service to a SOAP server.
- The undeploy function removes an existing SOAP service from a SOAP server.
- The list function lists all deployed SOAP services.

For our example, we are going to use the command-line tools for deploying our service, which is implemented with the org.apache.soap.server.ServiceManagerClient class. Using the ServiceManagerClient is very easy, and we will walk through each of its functions in this section.

NOTE *As we cover the following commands, you should note that each command references a servlet named* rpcrouter. *This servlet is at the core of all SOAP actions. It performs all service management and execution.*

list

The first function of the ServiceManagerClient that we are going to use is the list command, which lists all of the currently deployed services. To execute the list command, type the following:

```
java org.apache.soap.server.ServiceManagerClient
  http://localhost:8080/soap/servlet/rpcrouter list
```

If you execute this command, you should get a response that shows no deployed services. Examining this command reveals that it executes the Java application ServiceManagerClient with two parameters. The first parameter points to the SOAP server, and the second is the actual command to perform, which in this case is the list command.

deploy

The next command that we are going to perform will deploy our service to the SOAP server. This command also uses the ServiceManagerClient with the deployment descriptor describing the SOAP service. To deploy our service, execute the following command:

```
java org.apache.soap.server.ServiceManagerClient
  http://localhost:8080/soap/servlet/rpcrouter
  deploy DeploymentDescriptor.xml
```

This command takes three parameters: the URL to the SOAP server, the command `deploy`, and the file containing our deployment descriptor. After you have executed this command, execute the `list` command. You should now see output listing the `urn:apressserver`, which is the ID of our service. You can also view this service from the Web admin tool by opening your browser to the following URL and clicking on the List button:

```
http://localhost:8080/soap/admin/index.html
```

You should now see a page similar to that shown in Figure 12-3, which lists the name of our published service.

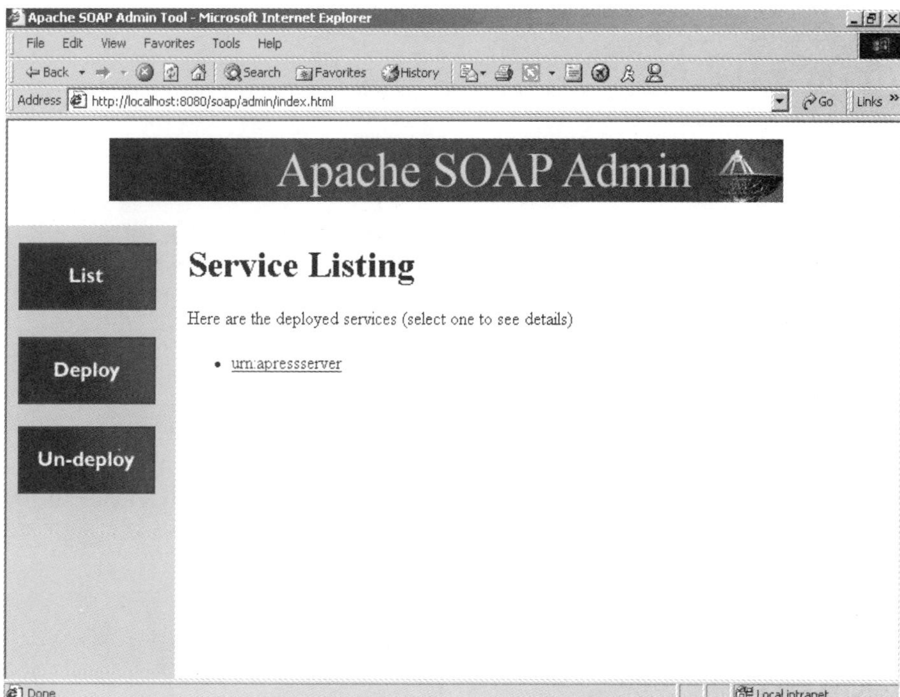

Figure 12-3. The Web presentation of the `list` *command*

If you select the service name, you'll see the details of the service, which should look similar to those in Figure 12-4.

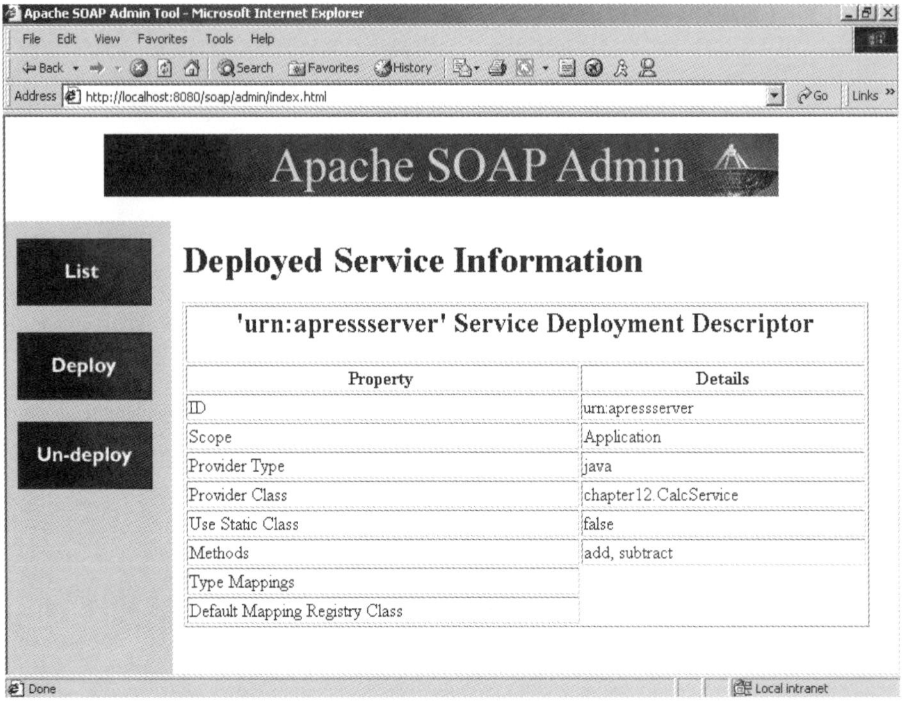

Figure 12-4. The detailed view of the `urn:apressserver` *service*

undeploy

The final function of the `ServiceManagerClient` that we are going to examine is the `undeploy` command. As its name implies, this command removes a previously deployed service. To execute the `undeploy` command, type the following line:

```
java org.apache.soap.server.ServiceManagerClient
  http://localhost:8080/soap/servlet/rpcrouter  undeploy urn:apressserver
```

The `undeploy` command takes three parameters. The first parameter points to the SOAP server and the second is the actual command to perform, which in this case is the `undeploy` command. The final parameter is the name of the service to remove.

SOAP Clients

Now that we have a service defined and deployed, let's write a client that executes one of the service's methods. The Apache SOAP project provides a client-side

API that makes it relatively simple to create SOAP clients. An example client, which we will use to execute one of our methods, can be found in Listing 12-3.

Listing 12-3. An Example SOAP Client `CalcClient.java`

```
package chapter12;

import java.io.*;
import java.net.*;
import java.util.*;
import org.apache.soap.*;
import org.apache.soap.rpc.*;

public class CalcClient {

  public static void main(String[] args) throws Exception {

    URL url = new URL ("http://localhost:8080/soap/servlet/rpcrouter");

    Integer p1 = new Integer(args[0]);
    Integer p2 = new Integer(args[1]);

    // Build the call.
    Call call = new Call();
    call.setTargetObjectURI("urn:apressserver");
    call.setMethodName("subtract");
    call.setEncodingStyleURI(Constants.NS_URI_SOAP_ENC);
    Vector params = new Vector();
    params.addElement(new Parameter("p1", Integer.class, p1, null));
    params.addElement(new Parameter("p2", Integer.class, p2, null));
    call.setParams (params);

    // make the call: note that the action URI is empty because the
    // XML-SOAP rpc router does not need this. This may change in the
    // future.
    Response resp = call.invoke(url, "" );

    // Check the response.
    if ( resp.generatedFault() ) {

      Fault fault = resp.getFault ();
      System.out.println("Ouch, the call failed: ");
      System.out.println("  Fault Code   = " + fault.getFaultCode());
```

```
        System.out.println("  Fault String = " + fault.getFaultString());
      }
      else {

        Parameter result = resp.getReturnValue();
        System.out.println(result.getValue());
      }
    }
}
```

This client follows a simple process that is common to most SOAP RPC clients: it first creates a URL that points to the `rpcrouter`, which we noted earlier, on our `localhost`. This is done in the following code snippet:

```
URL url = new URL ("http://localhost:8080/soap/servlet/rpcrouter");
```

The next step, performed by the client application, is to parse the arguments from the command line. These values are passed to the SOAP service in a subsequent method. The values created are `Integers`.

After the client has parsed to command-line arguments, it creates an instance of an `org.apache.soap.rpc.RPCMessage.Call`. The `Call` object is the main interface used when executing a SOAP RPC invocation.

To use the `Call` object, we need to first tell it which service we want to use. We do this by calling the `setTargetObjectURI`, passing it the name of the service that we want to execute. We then set the name of the service method we want to execute using the `setMethodName()` method, with the name of the method we want to execute. The next step is to set the encoding style used in the RPC call. We are using the value `NS_URI_SOAP_ENC`, which is the default URI encoding style used by a SOAP client.

The final step is to add the parameters that are expected when executing the named method. This is done by creating a `Vector` of `Parameter` objects and adding them to the `Call` object using the `setParams()` method. All of these steps are completed using the following code snippet:

```
Call call = new Call();
call.setTargetObjectURI("urn:apressserver");
call.setMethodName("subtract");
call.setEncodingStyleURI(Constants.NS_URI_SOAP_ENC);
Vector params = new Vector();
params.addElement(new Parameter("p1", Integer.class, p1, null));
params.addElement(new Parameter("p2", Integer.class, p2, null));
call.setParams (params);
```

The next step performed by the client application is to actually call the service method that we are interested in. This is done using the `invoke()` method with the `URL` that we created earlier. The snippet of code calling the `invoke()` method is:

```
Response resp = call.invoke(url, "" );
```

Notice that the return value of the `invoke()` method is a `Response` object. The `Response` object returns two very important items: error code and the value returned from the executed service method. You check for an error by calling the `generatedFault()` method, which returns `true` if there were an error returned and then you can check the `getFault()` method. If `generatedFault()` returns false, you can then get the value returned in the `Response` object by using the `Response.getReturnValue()` method. The following code snippet shows how you should process the response of an `invoke()`:

```
if ( resp.generatedFault() ) {
  Fault fault = resp.getFault();
  System.out.println("The call failed: ");
  System.out.println("  Fault Code   = " + fault.getFaultCode());
  System.out.println("  Fault String = " + fault.getFaultString());
}
else {

  Parameter result = resp.getReturnValue();
  System.out.println(result.getValue());
}
```

That is all there is to it. To test your client and service, compile the client and execute it using the command line:

```
java chapter12.CalcClient 98  90
```

NOTE *At this point, you should have the* `CalcService` *deployed and Tomcat should be running.*

Summary

In this chapter, we discussed the Apache-SOAP project. We described each of the steps involved in integrating SOAP into the Tomcat container, and we concluded by creating a sample SOAP application that was hosted by Tomcat. In the next chapter, we discuss how the XML Apache Soap project can be integrated into Tomcat.

APPENDIX A

The *server.xml* File

IN THIS APPENDIX, we discuss the server.xml file. This file can be considered the heart of Tomcat, and it allows you to completely configure Tomcat using an XML descriptor. We then describe the file's two major configurable Tomcat components: containers and connectors. Listing A-1 contains the source code of the default server.xml file, with all comments stripped out for clarity.

Listing A-1. The Source Code of the Default server.xml *File*

```
<Server port="8005" shutdown="SHUTDOWN" debug="0">

  <Service name="Tomcat-Standalone">

    <Connector className="org.apache.catalina.connector.http.HttpConnector"
      port="8080" minProcessors="5" maxProcessors="75"
      enableLookups="true" redirectPort="8443"
      acceptCount="10" debug="0" connectionTimeout="60000"/>

    <Engine name="Standalone" defaultHost="localhost" debug="0">

      <Logger className="org.apache.catalina.logger.FileLogger"
        prefix="catalina_log." suffix=".txt"
        timestamp="true"/>

      <Realm className="org.apache.catalina.realm.MemoryRealm" />

      <Host name="localhost" debug="0" appBase="webapps" unpackWARs="true">

        <Valve className="org.apache.catalina.valves.AccessLogValve"
          directory="logs"  prefix="localhost_access_log." suffix=".txt"
          pattern="common"/>

        <Logger className="org.apache.catalina.logger.FileLogger"
          directory="logs"  prefix="localhost_log." suffix=".txt"
          timestamp="true"/>

        <Context path="/examples" docBase="examples" debug="0"
```

```
          reloadable="true">

          <Logger className="org.apache.catalina.logger.FileLogger"
            prefix="localhost_examples_log." suffix=".txt"
            timestamp="true"/>

          <Ejb name="ejb/EmplRecord" type="Entity"
            home="com.wombat.empl.EmployeeRecordHome"
            remote="com.wombat.empl.EmployeeRecord"/>

          <Environment name="maxExemptions" type="java.lang.Integer"
            value="15"/>

          <Parameter name="context.param.name" value="context.param.value"
            override="false"/>

          <Resource name="jdbc/EmployeeAppDb" auth="SERVLET"
            type="javax.sql.DataSource"/>

          <ResourceParams name="jdbc/TestDB">
            <parameter><name>user</name><value>sa</value></parameter>
            <parameter><name>password</name><value></value></parameter>
            <parameter><name>driverClassName</name>
              <value>org.hsql.jdbcDriver</value></parameter>
            <parameter><name>driverName</name>
              <value>jdbc:HypersonicSQL:database</value></parameter>
          </ResourceParams>

          <Resource name="mail/session" auth="CONTAINER"
            type="javax.mail.Session"/>

          <ResourceParams name="mail/session">
            <parameter>
              <name>mail.smtp.host</name>
              <value>localhost</value>
            </parameter>
          </ResourceParams>
        </Context>

      </Host>

    </Engine>
```

```
  </Service>

  <Service name="Tomcat-Apache">

    <Connector className="org.apache.catalina.connector.warp.WarpConnector"
      port="8008" minProcessors="5" maxProcessors="75"
     enableLookups="true"
     acceptCount="10" debug="0"/>

    <Engine className="org.apache.catalina.connector.warp.WarpEngine"
     name="Apache" defaultHost="localhost" debug="0" appBase="webapps">

      <Logger className="org.apache.catalina.logger.FileLogger"
        prefix="apache_log." suffix=".txt"
        timestamp="true"/>

      <Realm className="org.apache.catalina.realm.MemoryRealm" />

    </Engine>

  </Service>
</Server>
```

Containers

Tomcat containers are objects that can execute requests received from a client and return responses to that client based on the original requests. Tomcat containers are of several types, each of which is configured within the server.xml based upon its type. In this section, we discuss the containers that are configured in the default server.xml file.

The <Server> Element

The first container element found in the server.xml file is the <Server> element, which represents the entire Catalina servlet container. It is used as a top-level element for a single Tomcat instance; it is a simple singleton element that represents the entire Tomcat JVM. It may contain one or more Service instances. The <Server> element is defined by the org.apache.catalina.Server interface. Table A-1 defines the possible attributes that can be set for the <Server> element.

Table A-1. The Attributes of the `<Server>` *Element*

ATTRIBUTE	DESCRIPTION
className	Names the fully qualified Java name of the class that implements the org.apache.catalina.Server interface. If no class name is specified, the implementation is used, which is the org.apache.catalina.core.StandardServer.
port	Names the TCP/IP port number on which the server listens for a shutdown command. The TCP/IP client that issues the shutdown command must be running on the same computer that is running Tomcat. This attribute is required.
shutdown	Defines the command string that must be received by the server on the named port to shut down Tomcat. This attribute is also required.

The `<Server>` defined in the server.xml file is contained in the following code snippet:

```
<Server className="org.apache.catalina.core.StandardServer"
  port="8005"
  shutdown="SHUTDOWN"
  debug="0">
```

NOTE *The* debug *attribute is available to all Tomcat elements. It states the debug level to use when logging messages to a defined* Logger. *We look at a* Logger *definition later in this appendix.*

The `<Server>` element cannot be configured as the child of any element. However, it can be configured as a parent to the `<Service>` element.

The <Service> Element

The next container element in the server.xml file is the `<Service>` element, which holds a collection of one or more `<Connector>` elements that share a single `<Engine>` element. *N*-number of `<Service>` elements may be nested inside a single `<Server>` element. The `<Service>` element is defined by the org.apache.catalina.Service interface. Table A-2 describes the `<Service>` element's attributes.

Table A-2. The Attributes of the <Service> *Element*

ATTRIBUTE	DESCRIPTION
className	Names the fully qualified Java name of the class that implements the org.apache.catalina.Service interface. If no class name is specified, the implementation will be used, which is the org.apache.catalina.core.StandardService.
name	Defines the display name of the defined service. This value is used in all Tomcat Logger messages.

Two <Service> definitions are found in the default server.xml file: a stand-alone Tomcat service that handles all direct requests received by Tomcat:

```
<Service name="Tomcat-Standalone">
```

and a service defined to handle all requests that have been forwarded by the Apache Web server:

```
<Service name="Tomcat-Apache">
```

The <Service> element can be configured as a child of the <Server> element, and it can be configured as a parent to the <Connector> and <Engine> elements.

The <Engine> Element

The third container element in the server.xml file is the <Engine> element, which represents the request-processing mechanism for a given <Service>. Each defined <Service> can have only one <Engine> element, and this single <Engine> component receives all requests received by all of the defined <Connector> components. The <Engine> element must be nested immediately after the <Connector> elements, inside its owning <Service> element.

The <Engine> element is defined by the org.apache.catalina.Engine interface. Table A-3 describes the possible <Engine> element attributes.

Table A-3. The Attributes of the `<Engine>` *Element*

ATTRIBUTE	DESCRIPTION
className	Names the fully qualified Java name of the class that implements the org.apache.catalina.Engine interface. If no class name is specified, the implementation is used, which is the org.apache.catalina.core.StandardEngine.
defaultHost	Names the host name to which all requests are defaulted if not otherwise named. The named host must be defined by a child <Host> element.
name	Defines the logical name of this engine. The name selected is arbitrary, but required.

The following code snippet contains the <Engine> element defined in the server.xml file. The element defines an engine named Standalone with a default host of localhost:

```
<Engine name="Standalone" defaultHost="localhost" debug="0">
```

The <Engine> element can be configured as a child of the <Service> element, and as a parent to the following elements:

- <Logger>
- <Realm>
- <Valve>
- <Host>

NOTE *All* Valves *that perform request processing and are nested in an* <Engine> *are executed for every request received from every* <Connector> *configured within this service.*

The <Host> Element

The <Host> element defines the virtual hosts that are contained in each instance of a Catalina <Engine>. Each <Host> can be a parent to one or more Web applications, each being represented by a <Context> component (which is described in the following section).

You must define at least one <Host> for each Engine element. This <Host> is usually named localhost. The possible attributes for the <Host> element are described in Table A-4.

Table A-4. The Attributes of the <Host> *Element*

ATTRIBUTE	DESCRIPTION
className	Names the fully qualified Java name of the class that implements the org.apache.catalina.Host interface. If no class name is specified, the implementation is used, which is the org.apache.catalina.core.StandardHost.
appBase	Defines the directory for this virtual host. This directory is the pathname of the Web applications to be executed in this virtual host. This value can be either an absolute path or a path that is relative to the <CATALINA_HOME> directory. If this value is not specified, the relative value webapps is used.
unpackWARs	Determines if WAR files should be unpacked or run directly from the WAR file. If not specified, the default value is true.
name	Defines the hostname of this virtual host. This attribute is required and must be unique among the virtual hosts running in this servlet container.

The <Host> element defined for the Standalone <Engine> is listed in the following code snippet:

```
<Host name="localhost" debug="0" appBase="webapps" unpackWARs="true">
```

The host definition defines a host named localhost that can be accessed by opening the URL:

```
http://localhost:8080/
```

The <Host> element is configured as a child of the <Engine> element, and as a parent to the following elements:

- `<Logger>`
- `<Realm>`
- `<Valve>`
- `<Context>`

The <Context> Element

The <Context> element is the most commonly used container in the server.xml file. It represents an individual Web application that is running within a defined <Host>. Any number of contexts can be defined within a <Host>, but each <Context> definition must have a unique context path, which is defined by the path attribute. The possible attributes for the <Context> element are described in Table A-5.

Table A-5. The Attributes of the <Context> *Element*

ATTRIBUTE	DESCRIPTION
className	Names the fully qualified Java name of the class that implements the org.apache.catalina.Context interface. If no class name is specified, the implementation is used, which is the org.apache.catalina.core.StandardContext.
cookies	Determines if you want cookies to be used for a session identifier. The default value is true.
crossContext	If set to true, allows the ServletContext.getContext() method to successfully return the ServletContext for other Web applications running in the same host. The default value is false, which prevents the access of cross context access.
docBase	Defines the directory for the Web application associated with this <Context>. This is the pathname of a directory that contains the resources for the Web application.
path	Defines the context path for this Web application. This value must be unique for each <Context> defined in a given <Host>.
reloadable	If set to true, causes Tomcat to check for class changes in the WEB-INF/classes/ and WEB-INF/lib directories. If these classes have changed, the application owning these classes is automatically reloaded. This feature should be used only during development. Setting this attribute to true causes severe performance degradation and therefore should be set to false in a production environment.

Table A-5. The Attributes of the <Context> *Element (continued)*

ATTRIBUTE	DESCRIPTION
wrapperClass	Defines the Java name of the org.apache.catalina.Wrapper implementation class that is used to wrap servlets managed by this Context. If not specified, the standard value org.apache.catalina.core.StandardWrapper is used.
useNaming	Should be set to true (the default) if you wish to have Catalina enable JNDI.
override	Should be set to true, if you wish to override the DefaultContext configuration. The default value is false.
workDir	Defines the pathname to a scratch directory that this Context uses for temporary read and write access. The directory is made visible as a servlet context attribute of type java.io.File, with the standard key of java.servlet.context.tempdir. If this value is not specified, Tomcat uses the work directory.

The <Context> element that defines the /examples application is included in the following code snippet:

```
<Context path="/examples" docBase="examples" debug="0"
  reloadable="true">
```

The context definition defines a Web application named /examples that has all of its resources stored in the relative directory examples. This context also states that this application is reloaded when class file are changed.

The <Context> element is configured as a child of the <Host> element, and as a parent to the following elements:

- <Logger>
- <Loader>
- <Realm>
- <Manager>
- <Ejb>
- <Environment>

- `<Parameter>`
- `<Resource>`
- `<ResourceParams>`

NOTE *If you do not have special configuration needs, you can use the default context configuration that is described in the default* `web.xml` *file, which can be found in the* `<CATALINA_HOME>/conf/` *directory.*

Connectors

The next type of element found in the `server.xml` file is the `<Connector>` element. The `<Connector>` element defines the class that does the actual handling requests and responses to and from a calling client application. The `<Connector>` element is defined by the `org.apache.catalina.Connector` interface. Table A-6 describes the `<Connector>` element's attributes.

Table A-6. The Attributes of the `<Connector>` *Element*

ATTRIBUTE	DESCRIPTION
className	Names the fully qualified Java name of the class that implements the `org.apache.catalina.Connector` interface. The `className` attribute is a required attribute.
enableLookups	Determines whether DNS lookups are enabled. The default value for this attribute is `true`. When DNS lookups are enabled, an application calling `request.getRemoteHost()` is returned the domain name of the calling client. Enabling DNS lookups can adversely affect performance. Therefore, this value should most often be set to `false`.
redirectPort	Names the TCP/IP port number to which a request should be redirected, if it comes in on a non-SSL port and is subject to a security constraint with a transport guarantee that requires SSL

The `<Connector>` element is configured as a child of the `<Service>` element, and cannot be configured as a parent to any element.

The HTTP Connector

Two <Connector> definitions can be found in the default server.xml file. The first is an HTTP connector that handles all direct HTTP request received by Tomcat. These attributes are specific to the HttpConnector. Table A-7 describes the possible attributes of the HttpConnector.

Table A-7. The <Connector> *Attributes Defined by the* HttpConnector

ATTRIBUTE	DESCRIPTION
port	Names the TCP/IP port number on which the connector listens for requests. The default value is 8080.
address	Used for servers with more than one IP address. It specifies which address is used for listening on the specified port. If this attribute is not specified, this named port number is used on all IP addresses associated with this server.
bufferSize	Specifies the size, in bytes, of the buffer to be provided for use by input streams created by this connector. Increasing the buffer size can improve performance, but at the expense of higher memory usage. The default value is 2048 bytes.
className	Names the fully qualified Java name of the HTTP connector class. This value must equal org.apache.catalina.connector.http.HttpConnector.
enableLookups	Same for all connectors.
proxyName	Specifies the server name to use if this instance of Tomcat is behind a firewall. This attribute is optional.
proxyPort	Specifies the HTTP port to use if this instance of Tomcat is behind a firewall. Also an optional attribute.
minProcessors	Defines the minimum number of processors, or instances, to start at initialization time. The default value is 5.
maxProcessors	Defines the maximum number of allowed processors, or instances, that can be started. The default value is 20. An unlimited number of processors can be started if the value of the maxProcessors attribute is set to a number that is less than zero.
acceptCount	Specifies the number of requests that can be queued on the listening port. The default value is 10.
connectionTimeout	Defines the time, in milliseconds, before a request terminates. The default value is 60000 milliseconds. To disable connection timeouts, the connectionTimeout value should be set to -1.

The following code snippet is an example `<Connector>` defining an HTTP connector:

```
<Connector className="org.apache.catalina.connector.http.HttpConnector"
  port="8080"
  minProcessors="5"
  maxProcessors="75"
  enableLookups="true"
  redirectPort="8443"
  acceptCount="10"
  debug="0"
  connectionTimeout="60000"/>
```

The Warp Connector

The second defined `<Connector>` is a Warp connector. The Warp connector handles requests that have been forwarded by a server, like the Apache Web server, that sits in front of Tomcat. An example `<Connector>` defining a Warp connector is contained in the following code snippet:

```
<Connector className="org.apache.catalina.connector.warp.WarpConnector"
  port="8008"
  enableLookups="true"
  acceptCount="10"
  debug="0"/>
```

The Warp connector can be configured using the set of attributes described in Table A-8.

Table A-8. The <Connector> *Attributes Defined by the* HttpConnector

ATTRIBUTE	DESCRIPTION
port	Names the TCP/IP port number on which the connector listens for requests. The default value is 8008.
address	Used for servers with more than one IP address. It specifies which address is used for listening on the specified port. If this attribute is not specified, this named port number is used on all IP addresses associated with this server.
className	Names the fully qualified Java name of the Warp connector class. This value must equal org.apache.catalina.connector.warp.WarpConnector.
enableLookups	Same for all connectors.
acceptCount	Specifies the number of requests that can be queued on the listening port. The default value is 10.

NOTE *The default* server.xml <Connector> *definition, describing a Warp connector, includes the attributes* minProcessors *and* maxProcessors, *whereas the class definition for* WarpConnector *does not define these attributes. This seems to be a simple oversight by the developers and does not appear to have any effect on the actual Warp connector.*

APPENDIX B

The *web.xml* File

IN THIS APPENDIX, we discuss the Web application deployment descriptor, or `web.xml` file. The `web.xml` file is an XML file, defined by the servlet specification, with the purpose of acting as a configuration file for a Web application. This file and its elements are completely independent of the Tomcat container. Listing B-1 contains a sample `web.xml` that we will be using, as an example, throughout this appendix.

Listing B-1. A Sample `web.xml` file

```
<?xml version="1.0" encoding="ISO-8859-1"?>

<!DOCTYPE web-app PUBLIC
  '-//Sun Microsystems, Inc.//DTD Web Application 2.3//EN'
  'http://java.sun.com/j2ee/dtds/web-app_2_3.dtd'>

<web-app>

  <!-- Define a Filter -->
  <filter>
    <filter-name>SampleFilter</filter-name>
    <filter-class>com.apress.SampleFilter</filter-class>
  </filter>

  <!-- Define a Mapping for the previous Filter -->
  <filter-mapping>
    <filter-name>SampleFilter</filter-name>
    <url-pattern>*.jsp</url-pattern>
  </filter-mapping>

  <!-- The define the login servlet -->
  <servlet>
    <servlet-name>login</servlet-name>
    <servlet-class>chapter2.login</servlet-class>
    <init-param>
      <param-name>paramName</param-name>
      <param-value>paramValue</param-value>
```

```
    </init-param>
    <load-on-startup>1</load-on-startup>
  </servlet>

  <!-- The mapping for the Controller servlet -->
  <servlet-mapping>
    <servlet-name>Controller</servlet-name>
    <url-pattern>*.ap</url-pattern>
  </servlet-mapping>

  <!-- Set the default session timeout (in minutes) -->
  <session-config>
    <session-timeout>30</session-timeout>
  </session-config>

  <!-- Establish the default list of welcome files -->
  <welcome-file-list>
    <welcome-file>login.jsp</welcome-file>
  </welcome-file-list>

  <!-- Define a Tag Library for this Application -->
  <taglib>
    <taglib-uri>/apress</taglib-uri>
    <taglib-location>/WEB-INF/lib/taglib.tld</taglib-location>
  </taglib>

  <!-- Define a Security Constraint on this Application -->
  <security-constraint>
    <web-resource-collection>
      <web-resource-name>Apress Application</web-resource-name>
      <url-pattern>/*</url-pattern>
    </web-resource-collection>
    <auth-constraint>
      <role-name>apressuser</role-name>
    </auth-constraint>
  </security-constraint>

  <!-- Define the Login Configuration for this Application -->
  <login-config>
    <auth-method>BASIC</auth-method>
    <realm-name>Apress Application</realm-name>
  </login-config>
</web-app>
```

The first several lines of the web.xml file will not often change. These elements define the XML version and the DTD for the web.xml file. The first line that is important to us is the <web-app> element because this element is the container for all Web application components. We will be examining the components that are the children of this element, but we won't examine every element of the deployment descriptor, which would be beyond the scope of this text. We'll examine only those elements that are most commonly used.

NOTE *All of the definitions that we add to the* web.xml *file must be added in the order of their appearance. If the order is changed, the Tomcat server will likely throw a SAXParseException.*

Adding a Servlet Filter

Servlet filters provide the necessary functionality to examine and transform the header information of both the request and response objects of a servlet container. To add a new servlet filter to a Web application, you must add a <filter> element and a <filter-mapping> element to the web.xml file. The following code snippet contains a sample filter entry:

```
<!-- Define a Filter -->
<filter>
  <filter-name>SampleFilter</filter-name>
  <filter-class>com.apress.SampleFilter</filter-class>
</filter>
```

This filter definition defines a filter named SampleFilter that is implemented in a class named com.apress.SampleFilter. The <filter> element's sub-elements can be found in Table B-1.

Table B-1. The <filter> *Sub-Elements*

SUB-ELEMENT	DESCRIPTION
<filter-name>	The string that is used to uniquely identify the servlet filter. It is used in the <filter-mapping> sub-element to identify the filter to be executed, when a defined URL pattern is requested.
<filter-class>	Names the fully qualified filter class to be executed when the string defined in the <filter-name> sub-element is referenced in the <filter-mapping> element

To deploy a filter, you must add a `<filter-mapping>` element. The `<filter-mapping>` describes the servlet filter to execute and the URL pattern that must be requested to execute the filter. The following code snippet contains a `<filter-mapping>` for the previous filter:

```
<!-- Define a Mapping for the previous Filter -->
<filter-mapping>
  <filter-name>SampleFilter</filter-name>
  <url-pattern>*.jsp</url-pattern>
</filter-mapping>
```

The sub-elements of the `<filter-mapping>` are described in Table B-2.

Table B-2. The `<filter-mapping>` Sub-Elements

SUB-ELEMENT	DESCRIPTION
`<filter-name>`	The string that names the servlet filter to execute when the defined URL pattern is requested
`<url-pattern>`	Defines the URL pattern that must be requested to execute the named servlet filter

NOTE *Make sure that the `<filter-name>` sub-element in both the `<filter>` and `<filter-mapping>` elements match. This is the link between these two elements.*

The result of these combined elements is a filter named `SampleFilter` that is executed whenever a JSP resource is requested in the application that owns this deployment descriptor.

Adding a Servlet Definition

The next Web component definition that we are going to add is a servlet. To do this, we use the `<servlet>` element and its sub-elements. The following code snippet contains a sample servlet definition:

```
<!-- Define a servlet -->
<servlet>
  <servlet-name>Controller</servlet-name>
  <servlet-class>com.apress.Controller</servlet-class>
```

```
  <init-param>
    <param-name>paramName</param-name>
    <param-value>paramValue</param-value>
  </init-param>
  <load-on-startup>0</load-on-startup>
</servlet>
```

The <servlet> sub-elements can be found in Table B-3.

Table B-3. The <servlet> *Sub-Elements*

SUB-ELEMENT	DESCRIPTION
<servlet-name>	The string that is used to uniquely identify the servlet. It is used in the <servlet-mapping> sub-element to identify the servlet to be executed, when a defined URL pattern is requested, if there is a <servlet-mapping> sub-element.
<servlet-class>	Names the fully qualified servlet class to be executed
<init-param>	Defines a name/value pair as an initialization parameter of the servlet. There can be any number of this optional sub-element. It also has two sub-elements of its own that define the name and value of the initialization parameter.
<load-on-startup>	Indicates that this servlet should be loaded when the Web application starts. If the value of this element is a negative integer, or if the element is not present, the container is open to load the servlet whenever it chooses. If the value is a positive integer or 0, the container guarantees that servlets with lower integer values are loaded before servlets with higher integer values.

After examining the sub-element definitions, you can see that this servlet element defines a servlet named `Controller` that is implemented in a class named `com.apress.Controller`. It has a single initialization parameter named `paramName`, with a value `paramValue`. It also is one of the first preloaded servlets when the Web application starts.

Adding a Servlet Mapping

The next Web component that we are going to add is a servlet mapping. A servlet mapping defines a mapping between a servlet and a URL pattern. To do this, we use the <servlet-mapping> element and its sub-elements. The following code snippet contains a sample servlet mapping definition:

```
<!-- The mapping for the Controller servlet -->
<servlet-mapping>
  <servlet-name>Controller</servlet-name>
  <url-pattern>*.ap</url-pattern>
</servlet-mapping>
```

The `<servlet-mapping>` sub-elements can be found in Table B-4.

Table B-4. The `<servlet-mapping>` Sub-Elements

SUB-ELEMENT	DESCRIPTION
`<servlet-name>`	The string that is used to uniquely identify the servlet that is executed when the following defined `<url-pattern>` is requested
`<url-pattern>`	Defines the URL pattern that must be matched to execute the servlet named in the `<servlet-name>` element

This previous servlet mapping states that the servlet named `Controller` is executed whenever a resource in this Web application, ending with `ap`, is requested.

Configuring the Session

The next Web component that we are going to add determines the life of each `HttpSession` in the current Web application. The following code snippet contains a sample session configuration:

```
<!-- Set the default session timeout (in minutes) -->
<session-config>
  <session-timeout>30</session-timeout>
</session-config>
```

The `<session-config>` element contains only one sub-element, `<session-timeout>`, which defines the length of time that an `HttpSession` object can remain inactive before the container marks it as invalid. The value must be an integer measured in minutes.

Adding a Welcome File List

We are now going to add a default list of files that will be loaded automatically when a Web application is referenced without a filename. An example `<welcome-file-list>` is contained in the following code snippet:

```
<!-- Establish the default list of welcome files -->
<welcome-file-list>
  <welcome-file>login.jsp</welcome-file>
  <welcome-file>index.html</welcome-file>
</welcome-file-list>
```

The `<welcome-file-list>` contains an ordered list of `<welcome-files>` sub-elements that contain the filenames to present to the user. The files are served in order of appearance and existence. In this example, the Web application first tries to serve up the `login.jsp` file. If this file does not exist in the Web application, the application tries to serve up the file `index.html`. If none of the files in the welcome list exists, an `HTTP 404 Not Found` error is returned.

Adding a Tag Library

Now we are going to add a tag library to our Web application using the `<taglib>` element. The following code snippet contains a sample `<taglib>` element:

```
<!-- Define a Tag Library for this Application -->
<taglib>
  <taglib-uri>/apress</taglib-uri>
  <taglib-location>/WEB-INF/lib/taglib.tld</taglib-location>
</taglib>
```

The `<taglib>` sub-elements can be found in Table B-5.

Table B-5. The `<taglib>` *Sub-Elements*

SUB-ELEMENT	DESCRIPTION
`<taglib-uri>`	Defines a URI that represents a unique key that the Web application can use to look up the defined tag library
`<taglib-location>`	Defines the location of the TLD representing this tag library

This entry in the `web.xml` file tells the Web application two things. First, it defines a unique key representing a tag library that can be used by a JSP in a container to identify this tag library, `/apress`. Second, it states the location of the tag library's TLD, which describes the complete tag library, as being in the file `/WEB-INF/lib/taglib.tld`.

Adding a Security Constraint

Next, we are going to add a security constraint to protect a resource in our Web application. The following code snippet contains a sample <security-constraint> element:

```
<!-- Define a Security Constraint on this Application -->
<security-constraint>
  <web-resource-collection>
    <web-resource-name>Apress Application</web-resource-name>
    <url-pattern>/*</url-pattern>
  </web-resource-collection>
  <auth-constraint>
    <role-name>apressuser</role-name>
  </auth-constraint>
</security-constraint>
```

The <security-constraint> sub-elements can be found in Table B-6.

Table B-6. The <security-constraint> *Sub-Elements*

SUB-ELEMENT	DESCRIPTION
<web-resource-collection>	Used to identify a subset of the resources and HTTP methods on those resources within a Web application to which a security constraint applies. The <web-resource-collection> sub-element contains two sub-elements of its own that are defined in Table B-7.
<auth-constraint>	Defines the user roles that should be permitted access to this resource collection. It contains a single sub-element, <role-name>, which defines the actual role name that has access to the defined constraint. If this value is set to an *, all roles have access to the constraint.

Table B-7. The <web-resource-collection> *Sub-Elements*

SUB-ELEMENT	DESCRIPTION
<web-resource-name>	Defines the name of this Web resource collection
<url-pattern>	Defines the URL pattern that will be protected by the resource

This security constraint protects the entire Apress Application Web application, allowing only users with a defined <role-name> of apressuser.

Adding a Login Config

To make a security constraint effective, you must define a method in which a user can log in to the defined constraint. To do this, you must add a login configuration component to the Web application. An example of this is contained in the following code snippet:

```
<!-- Define the Login Configuration for this Application -->
<login-config>
  <auth-method>BASIC</auth-method>
  <realm-name>Apress Application</realm-name>
</login-config>
```

The <login-config> sub-elements can be found in Table B-8.

Table B-8. The <login-config> *Sub-Elements*

SUB-ELEMENT	DESCRIPTION
<auth-method>	Used to configure the method by which the user is authenticated for this Web application. The possible values are BASIC, DIGEST, FORM, and CLIENT-CERT. If this value is set to FORM, the <form-login-config> sub-element must be defined.
<form-login-config>	Specifies the login and error page that should be used in FORM-based authentication. The sub-elements of the <form-login-config> are defined in Table B-9.
<realm-name>	Defines the name of the resource that this login configuration applies. This value must match a <web-resource-name> that was defined in a security constraint.

Table B-9. The `<form-login-config>` *Sub-Elements*

SUB-ELEMENT	DESCRIPTION
<form-login-page>	Defines the location and name of the page that will serve as the login page when using FORM-based authentication.
<form-error-page>	Defines the location and name of the page that will serve as the error page when a FORM-based login fails.

The results of this <login-config> sub-element definition states that the <web-resource-collection>, with a Web resource named Apress Application, uses a login method of BASIC authentication.

Index

D

E

F

G

H

I

X

Apress Titles

ISBN	PRICE	AUTHOR	TITLE
1-893115-73-9	$34.95	Abbott	Voice Enabling Web Applications: VoiceXML and Beyond
1-893115-01-1	$39.95	Appleman	Appleman's Win32 API Puzzle Book and Tutorial for Visual Basic Programmers
1-893115-23-2	$29.95	Appleman	How Computer Programming Works
1-893115-97-6	$39.95	Appleman	Moving to VB. NET: Strategies, Concepts, and Code
1-893115-09-7	$29.95	Baum	Dave Baum's Definitive Guide to LEGO MINDSTORMS
1-893115-84-4	$29.95	Baum, Gasperi, Hempel, and Villa	Extreme MINDSTORMS
1-893115-82-8	$59.95	Ben-Gan/Moreau	Advanced Transact-SQL for SQL Server 2000
1-893115-67-4	$49.95	Borge	Managing Enterprise Systems with the Windows Script Host
1-893115-47-X	$29.95	Christensen	Writing Cross-Browser XHTML and CSS2
1-893115-99-2	$39.95	Cornell/Morrison	Programming VB .NET: A Guide for Experienced Programmers
1-893115-71-2	$39.95	Ferguson	Mobile .NET
1-893115-90-9	$44.95	Finsel	The Handbook for Reluctant Database Administrators
1-893115-85-2	$34.95	Gilmore	A Programmer's Introduction to PHP 4.0
1-893115-36-4	$34.95	Goodwill	Apache Jakarta-Tomcat
1-893115-17-8	$59.95	Gross	A Programmer's Introduction to Windows DNA
1-893115-62-3	$39.95	Gunnerson	A Programmer's Introduction to C#, Second Edition
1-893115-10-0	$34.95	Holub	Taming Java Threads
1-893115-04-6	$34.95	Hyman/Vaddadi	Mike and Phani's Essential C++ Techniques
1-893115-50-X	$34.95	Knudsen	Wireless Java: Developing with Java 2, Micro Edition
1-893115-79-8	$49.95	Kofler	Definitive Guide to Excel VBA
1-893115-56-9	$39.95	Kofler	MySQL
1-893115-87-9	$39.95	Kurata	Doing Web Development: Client-Side Techniques
1-893115-75-5	$44.95	Kurniawan	Internet Programming with VB
1-893115-19-4	$49.95	Macdonald	Serious ADO: Universal Data Access with Visual Basic

ISBN	PRICE	AUTHOR	TITLE
1-893115-06-2	$39.95	Marquis/Smith	A Visual Basic 6.0 Programmer's Toolkit
1-893115-22-4	$27.95	McCarter	David McCarter's VB Tips and Techniques
1-893115-76-3	$49.95	Morrison	C++ For VB Programmers
1-893115-80-1	$39.95	Newmarch	A Programmer's Guide to Jini Technology
1-893115-58-5	$49.95	Oellermann	Architecting Web Services
1-893115-81-X	$39.95	Pike	SQL Server: Common Problems, Tested Solutions
1-893115-20-8	$34.95	Rischpater	Wireless Web Development
1-893115-93-3	$34.95	Rischpater	Wireless Web Development with PHP and WAP
1-893115-89-5	$59.95	Shemitz	Kylix: The Professional Developer's Guide and Reference
1-893115-40-2	$39.95	Sill	An Introduction to qmail
1-893115-24-0	$49.95	Sinclair	From Access to SQL Server
1-893115-94-1	$29.95	Spolsky	User Interface Design for Programmers
1-893115-53-4	$39.95	Sweeney	Visual Basic for Testers
1-893115-29-1	$44.95	Thomsen	Database Programming with Visual Basic .NET
1-893115-65-8	$39.95	Tiffany	Pocket PC Database Development with eMbedded Visual Basic
1-893115-59-3	$59.95	Troelsen	C# and the .NET Platform
1-893115-26-7	$59.95	Troelsen	Visual Basic .NET and the .NET Platform
1-893115-54-2	$49.95	Trueblood/Lovett	Data Mining and Statistical Analysis Using SQL
1-893115-16-X	$49.95	Vaughn	ADO Examples and Best Practices
1-893115-83-6	$44.95	Wells	Code Centric: T-SQL Programming with Stored Procedures and Triggers
1-893115-95-X	$49.95	Welschenbach	Cryptography in C and C++
1-893115-05-4	$39.95	Williamson	Writing Cross-Browser Dynamic HTML
1-893115-78-X	$49.95	Zukowski	Definitive Guide to Swing for Java 2, Second Edition
1-893115-92-5	$49.95	Zukowski	Java Collections

books for professionals by professionals™

About Apress

Apress, located in Berkeley, CA, is an innovative publishing company devoted to meeting the needs of existing and potential programming professionals. Simply put, the "A" in Apress stands for the "Author's Press™." Apress' unique author-centric approach to publishing grew from conversations between Dan Appleman and Gary Cornell, authors of best-selling, highly regarded computer books. In 1998, they set out to create a publishing company that emphasized quality above all else, a company with books that would be considered the best in their market. Dan and Gary's vision has resulted in over 30 widely acclaimed titles by some of the industry's leading software professionals.

Do You Have What It Takes to Write for Apress?

Apress is rapidly expanding its publishing program. If you can write and refuse to compromise on the quality of your work, if you believe in doing more than rehashing existing documentation, and if you're looking for opportunities and rewards that go far beyond those offered by traditional publishing houses, we want to hear from you!

Consider these innovations that we offer all of our authors:

- **Top royalties with *no* hidden switch statements**
  Authors typically only receive half of their normal royalty rate on foreign sales. In contrast, Apress' royalty rate remains the same for both foreign and domestic sales.

- **A mechanism for authors to obtain equity in Apress**
  Unlike the software industry, where stock options are essential to motivate and retain software professionals, the publishing industry has adhered to an outdated compensation model based on royalties alone. In the spirit of most software companies, Apress reserves a significant portion of its equity for authors.

- **Serious treatment of the technical review process**
  Each Apress book has a technical reviewing team whose remuneration depends in part on the success of the book since they too receive royalties.

Moreover, through a partnership with Springer-Verlag, one of the world's major publishing houses, Apress has significant venture capital behind it. Thus, we have the resources to produce the highest quality books *and* market them aggressively.

If you fit the model of the Apress author who can write a book that gives the "professional what he or she needs to know™," then please contact one of our Editorial Directors, Gary Cornell (gary_cornell@apress.com), Dan Appleman (dan_appleman@apress.com), Karen Watterson (karen_watterson@apress.com) or Jason Gilmore (jason_gilmore@apress.com) for more information.